the readers guide series

FINE ARTS

the readers guide series · editor K C Harrison MBE FLA

FINE ARTS

Jack Dove FLA FRCO ARCM

CLIVE BINGLEY *b* LONDON

FIRST PUBLISHED 1966 BY CLIVE BINGLEY LTD
16 PEMBRIDGE ROAD LONDON W11
SET IN 10 ON 12 POINT LINOTYPE TIMES ROMAN
AND PRINTED IN GREAT BRITAIN
BY THE CENTRAL PRESS (ABERDEEN) LTD

CONTENTS

INTRODUCTION

MY FIRST ATTEMPT must be to disarm criticism in advance by stating firmly the limits I have set myself in this book.

Fine arts is an enormously wide field, and I would never suggest that the following pages represent a comprehensive survey of the literature which the term encompasses. Such is not the intention of this book. On the contrary, I have tried to select from the mass of available literature some of the principal and most notable works, and to present a wide ranging introduction to the subject which might be useful to general readers and to librarians, both practising and student.

I may also say at once that music is already the subject of a readers guide in this series (by E T Bryant) and so I have excluded it completely from my book.

The proper compass of the term fine arts is no doubt open to debate, and I have drawn my own arbitrary lines around the subject to keep the size of this readers guide within easy bounds. Thus, for example, photography has been omitted, though I have no doubt that many people would consider it one of the fine arts. Generally, I have taken class 700 in Dewey's decimal classification scheme as a yardstick, although I have not, as the scheme requires, included subjects like town planning in my survey. Those who have themselves compiled selective bibliographies and book lists will know to what extent the author of a work like this is open to criticism for his omissions. I can only hope that this brief survey may be a useful introduction to the literature of the arts in the English language, and that such faults as it contains may more be matters of opinion than of fact.

I must acknowledge the help given by the librarian and his staff at the Victoria and Albert Museum in London, and by the Brighton reference library staff. I am grateful to Dorothy E Tunks and other members of my own staff for much assistance with detail; to Basil E Hunnisett, lecturer in the subject at the Brighton school of librarianship, for reading and criticising the manuscript. Dr A J Walford's *Guide to reference material* inevitably gave much help and I also read with profit Neville Carrick's *How to find out about the arts,* which I have tried, as far as possible, to avoid duplicating.

Jack Dove

GENERAL WORKS

1 BEFORE CONSIDERING the individual subjects which can be regarded as fine arts, it is worth looking first of all at some of the comprehensive volumes devoted to the arts in general in the form of dictionaries, encyclopedias, indexes, bibliographies and so on. Whereas, therefore, the rest of this book discusses the literature of fine art according to subject, this first chapter considers the more general works according to what librarians call their ' form '.

DICTIONARIES

Jules Adeline's art dictionary was originally translated from the French, enlarged in 1891, and reissued in New York in 1921. The latest edition (Michigan, Edwards) is dated 1953. It is confined to art terms and gives concise definitions of those used in painting, sculpture, architecture, etching, engraving, archaeology and heraldry. There are numerous line drawings on every page of the dictionary and definitions range from ' abaculus ' to ' zotheca '. It was a little disturbing to find ' impressionism ' described as the ' doctrine affected by impressionists ', but the day is saved by a proper description of the movement under ' impressionists '. On the assumption that basic terminology does not change, and bearing in mind that nothing of twentieth century art is covered, *Adeline* is a useful starting point for this survey.

A one-volume dictionary of 661 pages published by George Putnam's Sons, New York in 1943 is certainly worth mention. It was compiled by Albert E Wier and carries the title **Thesaurus of the arts.** The ten subjects covered are drama, music, radio, painting, screen, television, literature, sculpture, architecture and ballet. A book of this kind must take years in preparation and the author defines his objective as being to furnish concise, non-technical information regarding the personalities, subjects and terms connected with the fields of knowledge already mentioned. The pages of the thesaurus are in double columns, and small capitals in an entry refer to information at those subjects. For example:

Abacus—in architecture, the polygonal block forming the top of the CAPITAL of a COLUMN or a PILLAR.

Entries are brief but clear and this is a useful quick reference book to have at one's elbow. There are reading lists under various subjects at the end of the volume, arranged in order of title; unfortunately, these do not carry dates of publication of the numerous books cited.

Since Reginald Haggar's **Dictionary of art terms** (Oldbourne, 1963; NY, Hawthorne) undertakes not only painting, sculpture, engraving, etching, lithography and other art processes, but also architecture and even (rather surprisingly) heraldry, all in just over 400 pages, it is not surprising that it is sometimes rather cramped. This shows most in the longer entries on schools and styles—it is a little surprising to find Breughel cited without comment in the entry on ' mannerism ', for instance, or to be told that art nouveau originated in America with Sullivan's Auditorium Building (1888), though perhaps both views could be argued at length. The brief definitions are generally sound.

The books in the Everyman editions must be some of the most popular in existence and the very name appeals to the ordinary fellow who wants a reliable book on a subject. Since the publishers, Dent (Dutton in New York), established the Everyman's reference library series, some very valuable and handy volumes have been the result, including quotations, language dictionaries, an atlas and the *Everyman's encyclopaedia* itself. In 1962, William Gaunt, well-known art critic and historian, produced **Everyman's dictionary of pictorial art** in two volumes which sells for the modest price of 50s. In the introduction, the compiler says he has aimed to produce in concise form within the limit of 250,000 words and 1,000 illustrations, a handy reference to painters and periods, forms and techniques of pictorial art in all parts of the world where pictorial art has flourished from the earliest times to the present. Some 1,200 individual artists are mentioned. This is a dictionary in form, but the main coverage is: art forms and media; biographies of artists; descriptions of famous works; galleries and museums; periods and schools of painting; style and theory; technical terms. The standard of production is excellent and this book is a must for any fact-finder.

Peter and Linda Murray compiled **Dictionary of art and artists** in 1959; it was originally published as a Penguin and expanded and reissued in hard covers by Thames and Hudson in 1965. The import-

10

ance of reading preface notes to determine the scope of a book is amply demonstrated here. Over 1,000 artists are mentioned; there are over 1,200 illustrations; the book is restricted to painting, sculpture, drawing and other graphic processes, chiefly in western Europe and also in countries overseas in which the cultural forms and ideas of Europe have taken root; restriction in date is from 1300 onwards, meaning that medieval art is not covered. There are 220 pages devoted to the dictionary proper. Thereafter, another 210 pages of illustrations deal with techniques in colour and a visual history of art by countries. The two bibliographies form a short guide to art historical literature, the first by subject and the second alphabetical by author. As with all Thames and Hudson publications, this is a beautiful book to handle.

ENCYCLOPEDIAS

A major international project is the **Encyclopedia of world art,** in course of publication since 1959 by McGraw Hill for the Institute for Cultural Collaboration. This historical project covers the arts of all periods and countries, it is issued simultaneously in English and Italian and the eight volumes so far published run from 'A' to ' landscape architecture '. The encyclopedia covers representational arts in the broadest sense, including besides architecture, sculpture and painting, every other man-made object which enters the field of aesthetic judgment because of its form or decoration. No limits have been set on time, place or cultural environment, and the introduction stresses that this is a monographic work to be read rather than scanned and that the fifteenth volume will have a full and thorough analytical index.

Each volume is in two parts—the text and an exciting and generous collection of plates, including five-colour reproductions and modern photographs. These, like the articles, are in alphabetical order of subject. Artists are dealt with systematically—life, major works with dates and locations, and bibliography. A work of this nature is inevitably expensive to buy and, at more than £200 for the complete set of volumes, it will not be within the range of many private pockets.

Arthur Zaidenberg wrote an **Art students' encyclopaedia** in 1948 and it was published by Greenberg in New York. There are familiar terms lucidly described here with generous illustrations. For instance, abstract art, which is described as ' the purely linear features of a figure or object being secondary in importance to the needs of the entire picture ', has three illustrations. ' Action ' shows the human body at work and play, in five full-page sketches; and so on through the alphabet to ' wood block ', ' wood engraving ' and ' yellows '. This book is of particular interest and value to practising artists and art students, but the enquiring layman could also use it profitably.

The **Picture encyclopaedia of art** was first published in Brunswick, Germany in 1958 and was issued in an English edition by Thames and Hudson in 1960. It is in eight parts. The first is a general introduction dealing with the nature of art, its forms and styles. Six sections follow: antiquity, the middle ages, the renaissance, baroque and rococo, the nineteenth and twentieth centuries. A final section covers art outside Europe. There are sumptuous illustrations on all of the 564 pages, half of them in colour, and these include many works of art such as illuminated manuscripts, famous paintings, furniture and tapestries. Each section has a description of the period covered and this is followed by a comprehensive glossary of technical terms, movements in art, the names of artists and descriptions of their careers and works. The latter are apt to be missed, as they are not clearly defined. There is an index of 16 pages and this book, which is only a little above average size, is a mine of information and a joy to handle.

Louis Hourticq's **Encyclopaedia of art** in two volumes was published by George Harrap in 1938. The text is set in four columns to the page—an unusual style—there are many interspersed line-drawings and half-tone plates, and bibliographies to many of the entries. It is very comprehensive, generally concise in its information and is adequately cross-referenced, although necessarily selective.

For information on German art, a monumental encyclopedia, Otto Schmitt's **Reallexikon zur Deutschen Kunst-Geschichte,** has now reached volume five, as far as the word ' epitaph '. This was commenced in 1937 and as with other important voluminous German works, has progressed slowly, doubtless in part because of the war. Issued first in sections, these are then bound into volumes. Despite its German text, which tends to limit the encyclopedia's use in English-speaking countries, the parts so far issued, with their excellent illustrations and bibliographies, have proved the work's importance.

The **Dictionary of national biography,** as the standard work for British biography, should be remembered when details of artists' lives are sought. Gainsborough, for example, is written up by Cosmo Monkhouse and a bibliography is appended, now limited in date of course.

Similar comments apply to the **Dictionary of American biography,** where the personalities and achievements of subjects who have lived in the United States are described.

Of vital importance for contemporary purposes, or at least, for the last forty years is **Who's who in art,** first published in 1927, now in its twelfth edition (1964). The sub-title states that it contains ' biographies of leading men and women in the world of art today— artists, designers, craftsmen, critics, writers, teachers, collectors, and curators, with an appendix of signatures '. It is published by the Art Trade Press, in Eastbourne, UK and the advisory editor is well-known contemporary artist William Gear, who was curator of the Towner Art Gallery at Eastbourne from 1958 until his recent appointment as head of the department of fine art at the University of Birmingham. The first section describes the aims and activities of twenty eight academies, groups and societies, ranging from the Artists of Chelsea and the Federation of British Artists, to the Society of Scottish Artists and the United Society of Artists. The officers of each society are given. Then come the artists, nearly 4,000 of them. There are three appendices, one of monograms and signatures; a second which is an obituary, lacking many dates of birth and death; the third, a rather curious list of qualifications and abbreviations. Altogether, a most useful biographical dictionary in the artistic field in its broadest sense.

Who's who in American art (NY, Bowker) was first published in 1935 and went into its eighth edition in 1962. The editor is Dorothy B Gilbert and it includes Canadian, Alaskan and Hawaiian as well as American artists. There are nearly twice as many individuals as in *Who's who in art*.

The home of contemporary British art is acknowledged to be the Tate Gallery in London, and a meticulous and attractive catalogue of **Modern British paintings, drawings and sculpture in the Tate Gallery** by all British artists born in or after 1850 was published by the Oldbourne Press in 1964/5 in two volumes. It includes more than 1,500 works in the collection at the end of 1963, which represent about one third of the total held at the Tate. Further books will include artists born before 1765 and those born between 1765 and 1849. About 500 artists are included and the biographical notes on each are a rich source of information. The descriptions of the compositions themselves are also detailed, often including remarks made by the artists themselves. These catalogues will be chiefly useful for the information they give about each individual artist. At the end of volume two is a numerical index and an index of donors, and reproductions in colour and in black and white are given. Volume one covers artists from Edwin Austin Abbey to Lucy—a Canadian Eskimo artist—and volume two completes the alphabet.

Probably the US equivalent of the Tate Gallery is the Metropolitan Museum of Modern Art in New York, and the catalogues of public collections such as this, and of many notable private collections also, can be fruitful sources of information.

BIBLIOGRAPHIES

To the art student, the writer of books or periodical articles, the collector, the professor, the lecturer, the teacher and the practising artist, the **Guide to art reference books** by the librarian of the Fine Arts Library at Columbia University, M W Chamberlin, and published in 1959 by the American Library Association, is an invaluable book, albeit highly selective. What has been written on drawings, painting, sculpture, and architecture and how authoritative is it? What art periodicals are published and where are they indexed? What catalogues exist giving particulars of reproductions? What records of art sales are there? What reliable guides are there to art techniques, what directories, dictionaries and encyclopedias cover the arts? These and numerous other questions, can be answered from this bibliography which, although published in America, is international in scope. As far as libraries and series are concerned, however, English librarians will have to be circumspect for there is some American bias.

The lists of additions to the **Catalogue of the Victoria and Albert Museum** in London are published monthly. They are in alphabetical order of author, cover publications of all countries and because of this, are invaluable in enabling interested persons to pick up publications which may have escaped their notice through normal trade announcements. For instance, in one of the latest lists, produced in foolscap with replica catalogue entries, material is included from Moscow, Tokyo and Lillehammer. A most valuable bibliography which far transcends the bounds of national bibliographies and saves time in searching for important and essential material.

14

The Courtauld Institute's annual **Bibliography of the history of British art** 1934-1951, was a complete conspectus of publications in the field of British art. It can be profitably used by anyone but the varied demands of its users made continuation impossible and a gap has now been created by its discontinuation which needs to be filled.

YEARBOOKS

Since 1906 *Studio* magazine has published a regular yearbook in the field of interior furnishing and decoration. **Decorative art in modern interiors 1965/66** (Studio Vista, 1966) is the latest volume to appear and is a record of the year's achievements in the design of furniture, glass, ceramics, tableware, textiles and light fixtures. It is well nigh impossible to keep fully abreast of modern design and materials in all countries, but these yearbooks provide an excellent digest. They are not indexed.

This is a commercially produced yearbook, of course. It should be remembered that most professional associations, not only of artists, produce an annual yearbook or directory, but as these customarily concern association affairs and memberships, they more properly belong in the chapters devoted to individual arts subjects. They are always the logical first source of current information about contemporary artists and professional affairs.

In the year 1880, **The year's art** was first launched, describing itself as a concise epitome of all matters relating to the year's happenings in the arts of painting, sculpture, engraving and architecture, and in schools of design, together with information on events to come. Hutchinson were the publishers and publication lasted until 1948, when the yearbook ceased with the sixty-fourth volume covering the years 1945-1947. Although the format changed three times during the whole period, from small crown octavo to quarto, the pattern of content varied little. The national galleries and government activity; metropolitan galleries, art societies, clubs and schools; art at home, in the Commonwealth and the USA; art sales; art dealers and artists complete the inclusions. An index is provided to each volume and purchases under the Chantrey Bequest from 1877 are listed, all of which are housed at the Tate Gallery in London.

Illustrations are plentiful in all the volumes and the only impediment to their use and usefulness is that a reader must have some idea of when a particular event occurred, or when a particular artist practised. A cumulative index would have overcome this difficulty, but as comprehensive annual registers of events in the artistic world the volumes are still very valuable.

The multi-lingual **International directory of arts,** edited by Helmut Rauschenbusch, is published in Berlin by Deutsche Zentraldrückerei, and its seventh edition came in two volumes in 1963/64, but with a copyright date of 1958. Volume one, of 908 pages, covers: museums and art galleries, arranged primarily alphabetically by country; universities, academies and colleges, also alphabetically under countries; artists, restricted to active painters, sculptors and engravers, but in one alphabetical sequence of surname; restorers, again by country first; collectors alphabetically by surname, and associations under countries first.

The second volume, with 956 pages, has two main sequences— of art and antique dealers, and of galleries, or at least those not state or municipally supported. Smaller sections include: auctioneers, a very cursory list; art publishers of books, prints and postcards; art periodicals; antiquarian and art booksellers; and experts. All these sections have a prime division by country and are then arranged alphabetically by place with the exception of the experts, who are shown under their respective subjects, as archaeology, byzantine art and ethnology. There are page references here to other places in the volumes where the specialists are mentioned. The whole work is printed on art paper and there are a liberal number of illustrations of buildings, personnel and objects of art. The language is generally that of the country. This directory is a mine of factual information and a very ambitious project indeed.

The **International antiques yearbook** (Studio Vista) contains a widely divergent amount of information. The volume for 1965/66 has an account of the art sales of 1964, and five other articles on early furniture, glass collecting, Victoriana, Copenhagen porcelain, and hall-marking. Its factual content—and it is facts with which we are dealing—covers antique fairs at home and abroad; London antique dealers and booksellers; and an alphabetical list of towns in England and Wales giving the antique dealers in each, their addresses, telephone numbers and specialities. Some dealers in Scotland and Ireland, in European countries and in America, are also included.

The **Writers' and artists' year book** (Black) is an annual compendium for all who work in literary and artistic fields. For artists particularly, its sections on art agents and commercial art studios, societies and clubs, the markets for artists and designers and the graphic designer will be useful. Its main content is, of course, directed towards literature and the press.

TRADE GUIDES
With more and more interest in the values of works of art, **Art prices current** (Art Trade Press) assumes greater importance now than at any time in its 58 years' history. The auction galleries, especially in London and New York, are selling paintings at prices which have appreciated incredibly in a comparatively short time. This annual is expensive at twelve guineas. It is a record of sale prices at the principal London, continental and American auction rooms, part A dealing with paintings, drawings and miniatures and part B with engravings and prints, the two parts being bound together in one volume. The arrangement is chronologically by sale records from August to July of each year and the information is gleaned from sale catalogues.

The **Art-price annual** has been published in London since 1945/46. There are also German and French editions. It covers sales in Europe and the USA, but is very selective and can only give the outstanding items, so is not as useful as *Art prices current.*

The internationally famous London salerooms of Sotheby and Christie publish excellent **Catalogues** of the items they handle, as do the Parke-Bernet Galleries in New York, recently acquired by Sotheby. The catalogues are well illustrated and the provenance of each item is given wherever possible. They can be obtained for individual sales, or on an annual subscription basis, and priced catalogues can also be secured. It is a great pity there are no published indexes to the objets d'art which pass through these salerooms, but their illustrations in particular form very useful additions to a clippings file when suitably indexed. The catalogues are essential to anyone concerned with the identification, values, authenticity, or acquisition and disposal of artistic and antique items.

INDEXES
The H W Wilson Company of New York has rendered bibliographical services of immense value to librarians and researchers over the years in various fields, including biography, periodical literature and the output of books. The arts are also included in

their programme and since January 1929 they have issued their **Art index** which now comes four times a year in January, April, July, and October. These numbers are cumulated annually in September, and up to October 1953 were in three yearly cumulations. They now cumulate every two years. The emphasis is on American journals, but European periodicals are also covered. One fifth of the periodicals indexed are museum bulletins, nearly all American.

What nationality was Vanessa Bell and where was she born? Did she use a signature on her work and in which fields of art did she specialise? Daniel Trowbridge Mallett's **Index of artists: international-biographical** published in 1935 in New York (UK, Whitaker) with a supplementary volume issued in 1940 and reprinted in 1948, will answer such questions. But it also goes much further. It will direct you to other reference books where details of the artist's life and work can be found. The original volume includes 27,000 artists whilst the supplement (1940) contains an unspecified number of names not included in the initial volume. The indexes cover painters, sculptors, engravers, illustrators, and etchers whose works are exhibited in leading art galleries or who are besought by modern students.

For information about Irish or Welsh artists, there are two other useful indexes, but both published just before the first world war, so their usefulness is limited. W G Strickland's two volume **Dictionary of Irish artists** (Dublin, Maunsell, 1914) gives artists who not only were born in Ireland but worked there too. T M Rees's **Welsh painters, engravers and sculptors** (Caernarvon, c 1912) is a shorter book with about 150 biographies.

Where can you find a portrait of Johann Sebastian Bach, Mark Twain or Queen Caroline of Brunswick? These are questions which can be answered by the **Portrait index,** a book of sixteen hundred pages issued by the American Library Association in 1906. The 120,000 references to portraits cover some 45,000 people and it is not surprising that the work took ten years to compile. The subjects range from the illustrious to the obscure, and the only criticism is that twentieth century publications are obviously not covered. It would be a mammoth task to bring it up to date.

The **Repertoire d'art et d'archéologie** *depouillement des periodiques français et étrangers* was first published in 1910. It is a quarterly. The arrangement at first was alphabetically by country and, within countries, by names of journals. Now it comes annually and indexes every form of printed material on the arts, not just periodicals as was originally the case. The arrangement is still by countries then by subjects, and there are indexes of authors and artists annually. The only difficulty is the time lag in publication, as about four years elapse between the material indexed and the publication of the index. It appears, of course, in French.

PERIODICALS
An enormous range of magazines devoted to the arts is published in the English language, and it is obviously not possible to mention more than a few of the best known. One of the newest British journals is **Art and artists,** a monthly publication started in 1966 which, although as yet untried, is adopting a more popular approach to its subject than is usually the case with art journals. It is published by Hansom Books in London.

Perhaps the best known of the serious journals is **Studio** an illustrated publication devoted to fine and applied art, which first appeared in 1893. It is now published each month in London by Prism Publications and carries colour illustrations. Since 1908 each volume has carried its own index and there have been no cumulations.

The **Burlington magazine** for connoisseurs has been published monthly since 1903, and is an academic journal. Two or three long articles usually dominate each issue and they accompany shorter notices of the international scene and excellent critical reviews of the literature of art, as well as details of current events and the important acquisitions of museums. Illustrations, some in colour, are of a high standard and discerning quality, and all in all, this is a prime source for research workers. There is an annual index.

The **Connoisseur** (National Magazine Co), an illustrated monthly magazine for collectors, was first issued in London in 1901. Lavish in production standard, the journal covers the whole field of art with excellent illustrations, many in colour. International exhibitions receive extensive notices and exhibitions at important galleries in various capital cities are mentioned. There are book reviews and notes on the art market, and of course, the magazine is a happy hunting ground for advertisers of all nationalities. The six-monthly index includes an alphabetical list of articles under their titles and subjects, an alphabetical author list of contributors, and an author/

19

title list of books received or reviewed. Illustrations are indexed under their relevant subject, as architecture; arms and armour; artists, engravers and sculptors, and so on. There is a monthly index to advertisers and in each issue is a section *Connoisseur in America*.

Issued fortnightly since 1949 is the **Arts review** (Richard Gainsborough Periodicals), formerly **Art news and review,** of particular interest to artists and museum curators. It carries articles on modern art and artists and has crisp, signed notices of current exhibitions.

Apollo was first issued in 1925. A monthly magazine devoted to fine art, it is handsomely produced and carries book reviews, news of auctions and sales, and plenty of illustrations. It is a pity that this journal does not issue cumulative indexes, but its articles are indexed in the **British humanities index** and in the **Internationale Bibliographie der Zeitschriften literatur.**

The **Gazette des beaux arts:** *courier European de l'art et de la curiosité,* was first published in Paris in 1859 and still continues as a monthly. It is now in its sixth series. Indexes were published in 1885 to volumes I to XXII and in 1892 to volumes XXIII to XXXVIII. Tables of articles and illustrations to the first fifty volumes came in 1911 and 1915 respectively. Most articles are in French but occasionally some appear in English. A supplement bound in the magazine entitled *La chronique des arts,* published in Paris and New York (Wildenstein), gives news of museums and public buildings, under countries; collectors and collections; anniversaries, promotions and awards; congresses; exhibitions; book reviews.

Graphis (Sylvan Press), now in its twenty first volume, is published every two months in Switzerland and subtitled *The international journal of graphic and applied art.* The magazine is beautifully produced with top quality illustrations, and has its contents in English, French and German. Annual indexes are bound in the final number each year.

Another well-known Swiss magazine is **Art international** published ten times a year and now in its tenth volume. Articles appear in the language of the country of origin and there are notes of exhibitions and chronicles from the capital and artistic cities of the world, including reports of important auctions. Lack of an index is a drawback for reliance on the monthly contents lists, called indexes, is hardly practicable as the years go by.

The **Journal of the Warburg and Courtauld Institute** has been published quarterly since 1931 by the Warburg Institute in the University of London. As would be expected, it is a scholarly journal, with articles ranging over the whole field of the arts. There is a general index, an index of manuscripts and an alphabetical list of contributors to each annual volume.

On the other side of the Atlantic, the **Art quarterly** has been published since 1938 by the Detroit Institute of Arts. The pattern has been fairly consistent throughout each issue: two or three lengthy articles; shorter notes; notes on old and modern drawings; archives of American art; accessions of American and Canadian museums; and recent important acquisitions of American collections. The contents notes do not always point to the final section which is concerned with recent publications in the field of art, international in scope. Illustrations are generous. Full use of this scholarly journal is hampered by the lack of an index. The **Art bulletin** is another quarterly, published by the College Art Association of America in New York since 1913. A list of the contributing institutions reveals the high standard of the content, surveying all fields of art. Articles are few but lengthy and the books reviewed are equally few in number but are criticised and assessed at length. There is an annual index in the December number and the *Bulletin* has a few illustrations. The index to the first twenty-one volumes, from 1913-1948, by Rosalie B Green was published separately in 1950.

Back in Britain, of interest to the architect, designer, town planner and the artist too, is **Architectural review,** first published in London in 1827. A voluminous journal, with many advertisements of modern materials and plant, the *review* is international in flavour and essential for anyone concerned with buildings and their decor. Illustrations are numerous and exciting and there is a half-yearly index. Articles and advertisements are separately paged.

Two London journals of particular interest to antique dealers and collectors are **Antique collector** and **Antique dealer and collectors guide.** The former was first issued in 1930, and has five or six articles in each of its two-monthly issues. The latter is similar in format but first appeared in 1946. It is a monthly publication which carries a few fine, coloured illustrations in each issue. There are book reviews, news of sales and exhibitions, and notes of acquisitions by the important galleries.

The conservation and repair of works of art is in itself a form of fine art. The cleaning and retouching of painting, the restoration of sculpture, the repair of porcelain all demand the highest level of skill and, indeed, loving care on the part of the restorer. Apart from technical skill in each medium and an eye for intricate details and variations of colour or design, a restorer of pictures, for example, needs considerable academic knowledge of his subjects, of the styles and periods of his artists and the materials which they used, for a good deal of informed detection is often necessary before a picture can be cleaned and restored to the form in which the original artist completed it.

H T Plenderleith's **Conservation of antiquities,** published by the Oxford University Press, is basically for museum personnel, especially the curator who has no scientific staff at his beck and call, and it is, in Britain, the official textbook of the Museums Association on the subject. It would, however, also be useful to the private collector, for here is accurate scientific information on how to cope with almost any kind of accident that may have befallen any kind of antique. For the purposes of the book, antiquities are divided into three kinds: those made of organic materials—skin, wood, and bone; those made of metals; and those made of siliceous and related materials—stone, ceramics and glass. The book tells how to restore them and how they should be conserved subsequently.

All information in this book is practical, and directions are clearly given, so that many of the cures could be effected by the private collector, given the correct equipment and a little courage.

Ralph Mayer, in **Artists' handbook of materials and techniques** (Faber, second edition 1964; NY, Viking) explains that he was engaged for many years on chemical research in the paint, varnish and pigment industries, then with the actual manufacture itself, and later still, as a consultant to artists, a lecturer and a painter. The lengthy chapters of this book cover pigments, oil, tempera, grounds for oil and tempera, watercolour, pastel, mural painting, the conservation of pictures, chemistry and miscellaneous material. This is a very thorough survey of the whole field.

The English publishing firm of Thames and Hudson have set a high standard in the publishing of books on the arts in recent years. A translation from the German *Die Maltechniken* is Kurt Herberts' **The complete book of artists' techniques** (1958; NY, Praeger). The book emerged from practical experiments carried out by the author and is in three parts: techniques mainly dependent on the support or ground, which include rock and wall paintings, sgraffito, majolica, porcelain painting, stained glass, glass painting, and painting on ivory; techniques mainly dependent on the material ie mosaic, charcoal, chalk, ink, watercolour, pastel, tempera, oils, pointillism, encaustic, lacquer and resin; techniques mainly dependent on the tools, including silverpoint, pencil, pen, woodcut, line engraving, etching, drypoint, mezzotint, aquatint and lithography. There are some magnificent illustrations, 80 in colour, 89 in monochrome and 28 drawings.

HISTORY OF ART

2 THE FIRST REFERENCE under this enormously wide heading is to an excellent series of Penguin publications which should particularly interest art historians as well as laymen, because they are published at comparatively modest prices and should be within the range of most pockets. It is hardly necessary to mention also the continuity value of a wide ranging series, which enables logical yet comprehensive study of a subject. The series in this case is the **Pelican history of art,** which is under the general editorship of Nikolaus Pevsner. The series began in 1953, and now contains more than a dozen volumes dealing with the history of art and architecture in different countries and periods.

Reasonably priced also, and attractive to handle is Margaret H Bulley's lavishly illustrated work, **Art and everyman** (Batsford, two volumes 1952). It describes itself as a basis for appreciation, and is a general introduction to the study of art of all types, ages and countries. There are 840 illustrations in black and white which an imaginary couple, John and Mary, consider with the seeing eyes of everyman. It is really an exercise in aesthetics by making comparisons, and the use of the indexes is strongly advised, for every artistic field is covered. The first volume is principally concerned with design, and the second with paintings and drawings, considered under such headings as beauty, substance, self-expression, and power. Commentaries are given on all the illustrations and these will provide the facts which enquirers and interested persons may wish to have. The volumes were originally published at 84s but a cheap edition was issued in 1964 at half this price.

In 1956, the *Connoisseur* began publication of a series of illustrated **Period guides** to the houses, decoration, furnishing and chattels of the classic periods. There are six volumes in all: Tudor period, 1500 to 1603; Stuart period, to 1714; early Georgian period, to 1760; late Georgian period, to 1810; regency period, to 1830; early Victorian period, to 1860. The books are each split up into sections concerned with architecture and interior decoration; furniture; painting and sculpture; silver and silver plate; pottery, porcelain and glass, domestic metalwork; textiles; costume; jewellery; music and musical instruments; bookbinding and printing.

Facts can be more easily obtained from some books than others—for example, dictionaries by their very nature and alphabetical arrangement present information in a lucid and generally brief way. Other books may be discursive, but can also be encyclopedic and factual. In the latter category can be put Arnold Hauser's **The social history of art** published in two volumes by Routledge and Kegan Paul in 1951 (NY, Knopf). This is a translation from the German, a stupendous achievement which covers the whole field from the stone age to the film age.

Art here is interpreted in its widest sense, to include the poem, the novel, the drama and music, as set against the social and political events of the day; and it is not confined to any particular country.

Ever since primitive man scratched his drawings on the walls of caves, the concept of art has embodied the natural expression of man's environment and the tempo of the times in which he lived; and this has continued throughout history, despite wars and strikes, political vicissitudes and religious disturbances. To know what the Indian, the Indonesian, the African and the Chinese have produced, what happened artistically in the stone age, what was produced in Mesopotamia, the middle east, in ancient America and in the south seas, consider a series of books launched in 1959 called **The art of the world** (Methuen). Moderately priced and with illustrations in colour, the books published to date are: Hermann Goetz *India*: *five thousand years of Indian art;* Frits A Wagner *Indonesia*: *the art of an island group;* Elsy Lenzinger *Africa*: *the art of the negro peoples;* Werner Speiser *China*: *spirit and society;* H G Bandi *The stone age;* Leonard Woolley *Mesopotamia and the middle east;* H-D Disselhoff and S Linné *Ancient America;* Alfred Buhler *Oceania and Australia*: *the art of the south seas.*

The whole field of art in both the ancient and modern worlds is surveyed by Joseph Pijoan in **A history of art** (Barcelona, Salvat Editores, second edition 1933). The first of the three volumes in which the work was issued emphasises the details and importance of the paleolithic period as represented by the cave paintings at Altamira and then discusses the art of the ancient world as a whole, with particular reference to Greece and Rome. The second volume gives a detailed study of medieval art in Europe and also includes

Byzantine, Romanesque and Moslem schools. The third volume completes the survey, covering the period from Pisano to Brancusi and Giotto to Picasso. Emphasis throughout the work is on the history of painting, sculpture and architecture rather than applied arts such as tapestry and ceramics. There are numerous illustrations throughout the text.

How many readers venturing into a new field for the first time, have been discouraged and irrevocably put off further efforts by too many details given in highly technical terms, pretentious jargon or simply by being 'talked down' to? If this has been your experience in the field of art, try again with **The story of art** by Ernst Hans Gombrich (Phaidon, eleventh edition 1966; NY, Graphic).

Here is a fascinating story presented in simple language, beautifully illustrated in colour, and black and white. The works discussed are placed in their historical setting, giving an understanding of the masters' artistic aims, and how they are related by imitation or contradiction to what has gone before. Personal comment and preference have been kept to a minimum, the intention being to give the reader an introduction to the great masters and encourage him to pursue in more detail later those which have especial appeal. Wherever possible the works discussed have been seen in the original. The fascinating story begins in prehistoric times and ends with Picasso, Chagall, and Henry Moore.

Long acclaimed the standard world history of art for the general reader is Helen Gardner's **Art through the ages,** first published in 1926 and now available in a fourth edition published by George Bell in 1959, revised by the department of the history of art at Yale University under the editorship of Sumner McK Crosby (NY, Harcourt). The book is in four parts: ancient, European, non-European and modern art, and grouping is by periods and countries under these divisions. There are more than 800 illustrations, of which 524 are new to the latest edition, as well as bibliographies at the end of each chapter, a glossary and a fine relative index.

H W Janson in **A history of art** (Thames and Hudson, 1962; NY, Abrams) surveys the visual arts from the dawn of history to the present day in a magnificently illustrated book, with more than 1,000 illustrations, including nearly eighty fine colour plates. The text is arranged chronologically in four sections: the ancient world; the middle ages; the renaissance, and the modern world.

26

The outline of art by Sir William Orpen was first published in 1923, and republished by Newnes in 1961 in a revision by Horace Shipp. The subject content, which originally embraced European painting and sculpture from the renaissance only, has been considerably widened to begin at prehistoric times and to cover the whole world. The illustrations are plentiful and these too, have been considerably improved upon in the latest edition.

Attention should also be drawn briefly to a recent Swiss series containing (so far) eight titles, published by the firm of Skira and called the **Art ideas history.** The emphasis of the series is on Europe from the eighteenth century forward.

To turn for a moment to a byway of art history, have you ever thought why the anchor, besides being the mariner's symbol, is also held to signify hope? Or why the circle, from ancient days, has been a symbol of eternity, or why the lotus lily symbolises life and revival? These questions, and hundreds more, are answered by Arnold Whittick in **Symbols, signs and their meaning** (Leonard Hill, 1960). Seals, flags, coins, inn signs, coats of arms, military badges, medals and trademarks, are all covered. A preface note states the intention of the book is to entertain the curiosity of the general reader, but goes on to mention its usefulness to artists and designers, and those interested in symbolic expression. Emphasis is on symbols of the west, with oriental examples in the minority.

Regional or national histories of art abound, for it is logical to treat so broad a subject either by country or by period or by both of these. In addition to titles already mentioned which follow these forms, a number of outstanding books should be mentioned by the countries which they cover.

Taking, first of all, Europe as a continent, consider Eberhard Hempel's **Baroque art and architecture in central Europe** (Penguin Books, 1965). The division of the text is by period first, then by country, and lastly by the three ingredient subjects of architecture, sculpture and painting, although for the years 1600-1682, the three subjects come first. The countries dealt with are Germany, Austria, Switzerland, Hungary, Czechoslovakia and Poland. There is a bibliography and many plates.

H Gerson and E H ten Kuile's **Art and architecture in Belgium 1600-1800** (Penguin Books, 1965) covers architecture, sculpture and painting. The two chapters on architecture and sculpture are written by Dr ten Kuile, professor of the history of art in the College of Technology at Delft, and also a member of the royal commission on historic monuments. Part two of the book, on painting, is by Dr Gerson, who is director of the Netherlands Institute for Art History at the Hague and has lectured at the Courtauld Institute of the University of London and at Columbia University, New York.

A full and scholarly account of the development of the visual arts as part of the general history of England is to be found in the eleven volumes of the **Oxford history of English art** (OUP), edited by T S R Boase. These excellent and highly readable volumes, encyclopedic in content, are as much concerned with buildings, and social events, as with the products of artists and writers, and they cover the complete span of history. Four of the eleven volumes are still to come.

On a slightly different tack, for a portrait of a famous personality from British history, whatever his or her walk of life, consult the four volume work **Historical portraits 1400-1850** by C R L Fletcher, H B Butler and E Walker (Oxford, Clarendon Press 1909-19). The portraits were photographed by Emery Walker and the lives of the subjects were written by Fletcher. The books are, in effect, a miniature illustrated dictionary of national biography as well as a history of England for 450 years.

One further work which deserves mention here is **The arts in early England** (Murray, six volumes 1903-37), which shows the cultural activity of Saxon times in relation to the life of the period. The author, Gerard Baldwin Brown, died before the completion of the work, which was finished (appropriately enough) by E H L Saxon. The six volumes, in seven books, were published from 1903-37 and have full indexes to each part and line drawings and photographs.

A fascinating book about French medieval art of all kinds is Joan Evans **Art in mediaeval France 987-1498** (OUP, 1948). Miss Evans seeks to show how it owed its forms to the needs of its various patrons. She describes the art created for the church, which commissioned vast quantities of material; for the nobles, who at first built castles purely for fortification purposes, but gradually began to make them beautiful with stained glass, tapestries, wall hangings and so on; for the trade guilds which similarly required adornments for their chapels; and for the public buildings, for the enjoyment of all the citizens using them.

Rudolf Wittowker's **Art and architecture in Italy 1600-1750** (Penguin Books, 1958) actually begins with the Council of Trent in 1585 and is in three parts covering the period up to 1750. The pattern follows that of the Pelican series already mentioned.

Professor George Heard Hamilton of Yale University, curator of modern art and of the Edwin Austin Abbey collection at Yale's art gallery, was entrusted with the **Art and architecture of Russia** (Penguin Books, 1954) for the same Pelican series. Geographically, the book is concerned with European Russia and covers a thousand years of architecture, painting and sculpture. The author says the book is a history of the formal structure of a national art rather than an exercise in criticism. The account terminates in 1917. Many of the excellent photographs are published for the first time.

In **Art and architecture in Spain and Portugal and their American dominions 1500-1800** (Penguin Books, 1962), Professors George Kubler and Martin Soria have placed their emphasis on metropolitan, provincial and folk art, and on art as a moral, social and aesthetic response to life. The book deals with architecture, sculpture and painting in, respectively, Spain, Spanish America, Portugal and Brazil.

The Pelican series coverage of the far and middle east is represented by **Art and architecture of Japan** by Robert Treat Paine and Alexander Soper (1955), which covers the period from earliest times to the mid-nineteenth century, and by **Art and architecture of the ancient orient** by Dr Henri Frankfort (1965). The latter book discusses the period from 3500 BC to 500 BC approximately, covering Mesopotamia, Asia Minor, the Hittites of the Levant, the Armenians and Phoenicians. In addition, Sherman Lee (director of the Cleveland Museum of Art and an authority on far eastern art) **A history of far eastern art** is a comprehensive and scholarly survey of art in that part of the Asian world from 2500 BC until 1850. This is another publication from Thames and Hudson with the usual high standard of illustrative plates.

George Kubler's book **Art and architecture in ancient America** (Penguin Books, 1959) deals with the development of the styles in architecture, sculpture and painting of the Mexican, Maya, and Andean peoples of ancient America. The period covered is from the earliest known works to the end of the Aztec and Inca empires in the sixteenth century. The book tries to explain works of art as such instead of using them to estimate the degree of civilisation as in archaeological books. The arrangement is by geographical regions in three main divisions: Mexico, Central America, and western South America. As well as architecture, sculpture, and painting, topics such as town planning, pottery, textiles, and jewellery are discussed under the guiding division of region and period. Four maps, three chronological tables, 248 half-tone illustrations, and 119 text figures appear, of which many portray little known sites, buildings, and objects.

Lastly, a brief mention of Professor D S Robertson's **A handbook of Greek and Roman architecture** (CUP, second edition 1943), which is essential reading for serious students.

PAINTERS AND PAINTING

3 ERIC McCOLVIN PREPARED a list of the best books on painting in 1934. It was in fact his thesis for the honours diploma of the Library Association and was called **Painting,** published by Grafton. Obviously, it is now dated as well as OP but in some respects, especially the historical coverage of various schools of painting, the bibliography is still useful and should be known.

Any mention of reference books on painting would be incomplete without the Skira monographs and the National Gallery (London) catalogues. The editions of Albert Skira in Geneva are of outstanding quality. Series include the **Great centuries of painting** and **Painting, colour, history,** covering the various schools—Dutch, Flemish, Italian, Spanish, impressionism and modern painting. In addition, there are numerous monographs on individual artists, and all the volumes are noteworthy for the splendid quality of their colour reproduction.

The National Gallery catalogues cover various schools of painting also, but are not illustrated. They have very thorough documentation of the paintings in the Gallery, however, and are therefore sources of indisputable reference.

It is no exaggeration to say that perhaps the most valuable dictionary of artists is Emmanuel Bénézit's **Dictionnaire critique et documentaire des peintres, sculpteurs, dessinateurs et graveurs** (Zwemmer, eight volumes 1948-55; NY, Hacker). Not only does the dictionary give pointed accounts of the lives of artists, but also locations of their most important works and prices realised at sales, with dates. Its comprehensiveness is its greatest asset for it has no restrictions in time or locality. There are some illustrations, specimen signatures, and monograms of anonymous artists at the end of each alphabetical sequence through the twenty-six letters of the alphabet. Very minor artists are included too. A working knowledge of French is required to get the maximum benefit from the encyclopedia.

Bryan's **Biographical and critical dictionary of painters and engravers** was first published in 1816 in two volumes. Since then, it has gone through four editions, the last being revised by G C Williamson in 1903/4 and reprinted in five volumes in 1964 by the Kennicat Press in New York. Less comprehensive than Bénézit, it often gives longer factual accounts of the lives of painters and engravers, and lists the locations of their most important works. A few monograms of artists are given throughout the whole sequence and they are cumulated at the end of volume five.

An encyclopedia of painting (NY, Crown; Hutchinson, 1956), international in scope, from prehistoric times to 1955, was edited by Bernard S Myers of the City College in New York. Here is an attempt to give a picture of the outstanding painters, movements, styles and techniques from ancient times to the present day. There are more than 1,000 illustrations, many of them in colour, although the standard of reproduction is uneven.

The most comprehensive of all dictionaries of painters and engravers is a German work edited by Ulrich Thième and Felix Becker **Allgemeines Lexikon der bildenden Künstler von der Antike bis zur Gegenwart.** This was published in thirty seven volumes from 1907 to 1950, a facsimile reprint was issued in 1964, and it includes artists living at the time. But contemporary artists are dealt with in Hans Vollmer's **Allgemeines Lexikon der bildenden Künstler des XX Jahrhunderts.** This is published in Leipzig in six volumes and the two works together give the most thorough and complete coverage of artists of all nations and periods. The articles in Thième and Becker are signed; in the Vollmer they are not, but of course the former was published over nearly half a century and necessarily, the bibliographies are not up to date and references to periodical articles are likewise lacking. Volume thirty seven, incidentally, is a supplementary volume of **Meister mit Notnamen** and has a concluding section of 82 pages on monograms and their attributions. Care must be taken in handling volumes. There are two sequences of entries, the first ending in volume five, where a second sequence begins, going from A - G. This is completed in volume six from H - Z and from a user's point of view, this second sequence is the most effective as it contains the more modern and contemporary artists. The bibliographies refer to articles in periodicals and there is a list of the abbreviations used at the beginning of volume one. For these encyclopedic works, a thorough working knowledge of the German language is necessary.

While on the subject of monograms, a **Monogram Lexikon** of painters since 1850 was prepared by Franz Goldstein and published in Berlin in 1964. The first 810 pages are in alphabetical order of monograms, the following 25 pages are of symbols, and then comes a full name index of the artists mentioned with their cyphers.

With foreign publications in mind, **Enciclopedia della pittura italiana,** edited in two volumes by Galetti and Ettore (1950), is one which deals especially with the lesser known works of the great Italian masters, and with lesser painters from the renaissance down to modern times. Locations are given, there are numerous illustrations and some autographs, but a knowledge of Italian is necessary.

A book which deals with art movements and artists from the time of the impressionists to those contemporary artists who first made their mark before the second world war, is C Lake and R Maillard **Dictionary of modern painting** (Methuen, second edition 1958; NY, Tudor). The entries are in alphabetical order and explain the significance of movements and artists, with plenty of illustrations.

To define one of the twentieth century artistic developments, abstract painting, is not easy, for its pattern and scope is constantly changing. Michael Seuphor (this is a pseudonym) has included in his **A dictionary of abstract painting** (Methuen, 1957; NY, Tudor) a history of the subject and the whole book is full of accurate and extensive detail. The English edition is translated from the original French and the colour illustrations are excellent.

Another specialist field of painting is covered in J J Foster's **Dictionary of painters of miniatures** (Philip Allan, 1926). The period covered is from Holbein to the mid-nineteenth century, and the author has taken 'miniature' to include all works of miniature size, not just head and shoulder portraits. The book includes artists in media other than paint who turned their hands to miniature work, and the author finished compiling it only a month before his death in 1923.

More limited in scope, but complete in its field is **British miniaturists** by Basil S Long (Bles, 1929), which gives biographical details of miniaturists working in Britain between the sixteenth and nineteenth centuries, and a list of towns where they worked.

M H Grant's **Dictionary of British landscape painters** (F Lewis,

1952) lists most of the British school working between 1600 and 1850, and seascape painters are also included.

Turning from types of painting, let us consider some of the works which relate to painters and painting in different countries. **Painting and sculpture in Europe from 1780-1880** (Penguin Books, 1960) is the subject of Fritz Novotny's treatise in the *Pelican history of art* series. As expected, painting occupies by far the largest part of the volume, starting with Jacques Louis David and classicism in France and proceeding to the impressionists. There are bibliographies and plates.

The richness of style and colour in the work of the Flemish artists is well to the fore in more than 900 plates, both coloured and monochrome, which constitute volume two of **Flemish painters 1430-1830** (Faber, 1960; NY, Viking) by R H Wilenski. The first volume is in two parts; the first shows in successive chapters the changing conditions, decade by decade, in the Netherlands; the painters who were working at any time during the period covered, either at home or abroad and the work on which they were engaged. The second part of volume one is a dictionary of some 2,500 Flemish painters from 1430-1900.

Wilenski has also covered the French scene in his two books **French painting** (Medici, 1950) and **Modern French painters** (Faber, fourth edition 1964; NY, Harcourt). Both these volumes are intended primarily for students.

The history and masters of French painting from the early times up to the year 1933 are presented in four volumes, issued in Paris between 1934-37, by Alfred Leroy under the title **Histoire de la peinture française.** The illustrations are poor but there is a good bibliography and an index of artists in each volume. A companion volume **Histoire de la peinture anglaise** was published in Paris in 1939.

Impressionism! 1855-1886 were the years, according to John Rewald, whose **History of impressionism** (Doubleday, revised edition 1961) was first published in 1946, although he points to the year of 1874 as the coming of age of this style of painting. Eleven chapters consider these thirty one eventful years stretching from Monet to Van Gogh, and the beginning of the post-impressionist era. Notes of sources are given at the end of each chapter; there is

34

a calendar of each year, showing the contemporary events which were taking place and the activities of each of the ten leading artists.

The same author's **Post-impressionism** (Doubleday) was published in 1956, and carries the story forward to 1893. The pattern of arrangement is as in the previous volume.

German painting of the fifteenth and sixteenth centuries is covered by Werner R Deusch in two handsome volumes published by Zwemmer **Deutsche Malerei des fünfzehnten Jahrhunderts** (1930) and **Deutsche Malerei des sechszehnten Jahrhunderts** (1936). The text is slight, and full page black and white reproductions of the country's famous paintings take up the bulk of each volume. There is an annotated list of the artists and pictures. The monochrome quality of the reproductions is excellent, but these intervening thirty years have witnessed great strides in colour reproduction, which may now restrict the value of these volumes.

British painting from Tudor times to 1900 (Medici, 1933) is surveyed in detail by C H Collins Baker, who was surveyor of the king's pictures and head of research in art history in the Huntington Library and Art Gallery, California. A chapter by Dr R Montague James, provost of Eton College, lengthens the period coverage by dealing with the medieval period.

English painters from William Hogarth to William Dyce are fully and critically treated by Richard and Samuel Redgrave in **A century of painters of the English school** (Sampson Low, two volumes 1866). Detailed contents of each chapter are given in the contents lists, and the outstanding artists such as Richard Wilson, Sir Joshua Reynolds and Sir Thomas Lawrence, are given lengthy treatment. There are no illustrations but for facts of lives and works, this is a must.

Between 1898 and 1907, Laurence Binyon compiled his **Catalogue of drawings by British artists and artists of foreign origin working in Great Britain in the British Museum,** an indispensable four volume work. Many important drawings have been added to the collections since, additional valuable information about several artists has been obtained and the British drawings in the museum have now been arranged on a chronological basis. Study of the history of the art of a particular period is thereby facilitated and the trustees decided that a new catalogue should be compiled. The first volumes appeared in 1960, one of text and the other of eight plates in colour and 297 in monochrome. These volumes cover the sixteenth and seventeenth centuries. The volume of text is in two parts, one for each century, and the anonymous drawings are listed first. Then follow details of the lives and works of all the artists represented, with bibliographies, their drawings and the history and attributions of each. There is a short handlist of foreign artists —that is artists with British connections—on pages 556-578, and three indexes—one of provenances (the history of a drawing, where acquired, when and by whom), the second listing works referred to, and the third being a subject index to the drawings under such headings as architecture, biblical, costume, jewellery and topography.

Another catalogue, published in 1927, but a very handy supplement to the dictionaries and encyclopedias of painters, is the Victoria and Albert Museum's **Catalogue of watercolour paintings** by British artists and foreigners working in Great Britain. These are works actually in the museum, whether in the permanent or the loan collections.

What famous and outstanding pictures are there in the national and municipal picture galleries of England, Scotland and Wales? Anthony Blunt's **The nation's pictures** (Chatto & Windus, 1950) will answer this question. It was originally planned for visitors to the United Kingdom but British residents will find it no less useful. Forty one galleries are mentioned, and the royal collections at Hampton Court, Windsor, Kensington and Holyrood.

In the same vein, Sir John Rothenstein's **The Tate Gallery** (Thames and Hudson, 1958) is a beautiful book, which gives the history of the gallery from its conception in 1890 through its inception in 1897 to the 1950's. The Tate is the largest art gallery in the British Commonwealth and has the national collection of British painting from the seventeenth century, as well as representative collections of modern painting and sculpture. Sir John chose the paintings and sculpture himself, and these are all described in detail. There are 68 reproductions in full colour and 39 in photogravure, with an index of painters and sculptors.

The first public exhibition of the works of English artists took place in 1760, organised by the Society of Artists, founded six years before. The history of this and the Free Society of Artists makes interesting reading in Algernon Graves' **The Society of Artists of Great Britain 1760-1791 and the Free Society of Artists 1761-1783**. The dictionary of artists exhibiting with these societies before the foundation of the Royal Academy provides probably the only easily accessible record of such exhibitions during this period. Similarly the author's **The British Institution 1806-1867** (published by himself) is a complete dictionary of contributors and their work during these years and is unusual in that the sizes of the pictures shown are quoted— important in identifying works. Add to these Algernon Graves' **The Royal Academy of Arts** and the author's coverage of exhibiting artists is pretty thorough to the beginning of this century. This particular set of eight volumes covers contributors and their work from the foundation of the academy in 1769 to 1904. The dates of exhibitions given enable you to go to the original exhibition catalogues for further information if necessary. It is a guide, not only to painters, well known and obscure, but also to the titles of their works and is particularly useful for tracing artists, competent but not nationally known.

There are nineteen volumes in Raimond Van Marle's **Development of the Italian schools of painting** (The Hague, Nijhoff 1923-28). This is a stupendous work by the erstwhile doctor of the faculty of letters of the University of Paris. Illustrations are plentiful and the indexes to each volume are thorough.

Prominent Dutch painters of the fifteenth and sixteenth centuries are listed in Max J Friedlander's **Early Netherlandish painting: from Van Eyck to Breughel** (Phaidon, 1956). In this edition the original German text has been translated and annotated by the editor, F Grossmann. There are some 300 illustrations, a dozen of them in colour.

The Dutch school of painting is less capable of formal analysis than, for example, the Italian school and has therefore been somewhat lacking in appeal for scholars. But what it lacks in erudition it makes up in precision and beauty, as is amply demonstrated in **Dutch painting** by J Leymarie (Geneva, Skira 1956), in which all the illustrations are in full colour. Many lesser known artists are included whose work is seldom reproduced.

A chronological **History of Spanish painting** (OUP) up to the period of the early renaissance has been produced by Chandler R Post, lecturer at Harvard University, in twelve volumes published between 1930-1958. Volume one contains a bibliography covering the first three volumes issued and there are specialised bibliographies in the later volumes; illustrations are in monochrome.

Now a word on technique. More people than ever today are wielding brush upon paper or canvas and Hilaire Hiler's **Notes on the technique of painting** (Faber, second edition 1954) is a very useful and comprehensive guide. On the title page appears an old Chinese saying: ' If the wrong man uses the right means, the right means work in the wrong way '. How to put canvas on a panel? How can it be stretched? How to prepare glue, colours, pigments, resin, oils, tempera, watercolours, varnishes, murals; selection and care of brushes; frescoes, easels and palettes. These and many more aspects are discussed.

The advantages of using garlic for culinary purposes are debatable. However, from Hesketh Hubbard's **Materia pictoria** (Pitman, second edition) we learn that it is invaluable to the painter when correctly used—for instance, in the preparation of amber varnish, to furnish moisture for evaporation. The book deals with the technical business of painting; the materials to use, and how to use them.

Reproductions are almost an artistic field of their own, and a valuable key is the **Index to reproductions of European paintings** by Isabel Stevenson Monro and Kate M Monro (H W Wilson, 1956). The index refers to reproductions in a total of 328 books. The American equivalent, by the same authors, is **Index to reproductions of American paintings** (H W Wilson, 1948—first supplement 1964).

A remarkable aid to the selection of reproductions is **Fine art reproductions of old and modern masters** (Soho Gallery, 1965). This exhaustive catalogue of the New York Graphic Society (who publish it in the USA) offers a glimpse of art history from Egyptian, Assyrian and classical art, down to the twentieth century. The book contains perhaps the largest selection of colour illustrations of fine paintings ever collated in a single volume, some 2,000.

On a less ambitious scale, but extremely useful are two catalogues of reproductions published by UNESCO covering the periods up to 1860 and from 1860-1965. Considerable annotation is given for each entry and there are monochrome illustrations. The title in each case is **Catalogue of colour reproductions of paintings** (HMSO, two volumes).

For the past six years the British Broadcasting Corporation has issued a coloured reproduction each month for use by listeners to the radio series *Painting of the month*. This year (1966) these are offered in more permanent form as a book, serving a dual purpose, as a straightforward study of, in this case, Dutch painting from the seventeenth to the twentieth century, and as a visual supplement to the radio programme. The twelve paintings forming the nucleus of the study are reproduced in colour with additional black and white illustrations and explanatory text by experts in this particular field. The issue of subsequent studies of various art schools in future years should provide valuable material for the student.

SCULPTURE

4 COMPARED WITH PAINTING, the literature concerned with sculpture is smaller, although, as will have been evident from the titles, some of the works cited in the previous three chapters have covered both painting and sculpture in their chosen fields.

First of all, a brief but concise account of the development of sculpture as a fine art form is **A history of sculpture** by George Henry Chase and Chandler R Post (Harper, 1934). The period covered is from the earliest times up to the year 1925, and this profusely illustrated book includes a glossary, indexes of sculptors, monuments and places, and full bibliographical notes at the end of each chapter.

More specific in scope is Arthur Gardner's **English medieval sculpture,** the second edition of which was published by Cambridge University Press in 1951, the book having first appeared in 1935. There are nearly 700 illustrations.

Leading on from this is the even more specialised field of **English church monuments.** Subtitled **an introduction to the study of tombs and effigies in the medieval period,** Frederick H Crossley's book (Batsford, new edition 1933) is a comprehensive study with a chronological list of effigies illustrated which shows the development of armour and costume. There is also a short chapter on brasses.

Katharine Esdaile's **English church monuments 1510-1840** (Batsford, 1946) is a fully illustrated survey of the ecclesiastical field, as yet too little recognised. In a long, illustrated introduction Sacheverell Sitwell deals with the transition period between gothic and renaissance art.

Monumental brasses were an integral part of medieval sculpture, and students can explore both this and the whole of medieval sculpture in Lawrence Stone's **Sculpture in Britain: the middle ages** (1955), yet another volume in the *Pelican history of art* series published by Penguin Books. The book is followed by Margaret Whinney **Sculpture in Britain 1530-1830** (Penguin Books, 1964).

Monumental brasses: the brasses of England (Allen & Unwin, seventh edition 1953) was written by Herbert W Macklin of St John's College, Cambridge, president of the Monumental Brass Society in 1907. Many people, especially students, indulge in brass rubbing as a hobby and this book describes the monumental brasses yet existing in England. These brasses are particularly useful to illustrate the costume of a period, be they military, ecclesiastical or civil, and the art of engraving them was prevalent from Edward I's reign in the thirteenth century to the beginning of the eighteenth century.

Although it was first published in 1926, **A list of monumental brasses in the British Isles** compiled by Mill Stephenson (Headley) still provides a valuable guide. Arranged by county and then by location within the county, the entries include information no longer available from the brass itself, with estimates of size and references to works in which illustrations of the brasses may be found.

'Art is a fruit which is born of man himself. But whereas all fruits have forms intrinsically their own . . . the human fruit we call "Art" nearly always embodies a ridiculous resemblance to something else.' Carola Giedion-Welcker quotes this thoughtful remark of the French sculptor Jean Arp as a protest against representational art in her book on **Contemporary sculpture** (Zwemmer, second edition 1961; NY, Wittenburn). Whether or not readers are converted to modern sculpture by this book they cannot fail to be interested by its intelligent and informative approach to the subject. Mrs Giedion-Welcker defends modern sculpture (and there is perhaps a need for her to defend, for there is no doubt that the majority of people prefer their art to make recognisable shapes) by showing that man has escaped from narrative—the result of classical narcissism which caused him to produce smooth, perfect reproductions of human figures—into symbolism, which is a purer emanation of the human mind; and, as a result of realising that he is not the centre of the universe, man has begun to appreciate the beauty of the materials he uses, and to let the wood, stone or other medium live and speak for itself. Those who have more confidence in their own opinions may ignore all this and refer straight to the photographs, which are accompanied where appropriate by quotations from the writings of the artists themselves, or their critics; or to the section which gives biographies of the most famous modern sculptors, in alphabetical order. There is also a lengthy bibliography at the end of the book.

Rupert Gunnis was a lover of the arts and a shrewd collector, who died just a short time ago. In 1953, he completed his **Dictionary of British sculptors 1660-1851** (Odhams, 1953), a work as unique as it is comprehensive and detailed, and which includes foreign sculptors who worked here. In fact, more than 1,700 individuals are mentioned. The book has lists of works accomplished and their present whereabouts. The author visited some 6,000 churches in Great Britain alone, itself a stupendous achievement. There is a comprehensive index of places, under towns and distinctive names, and an index of names also, which together have more than 12,000 entries. This is the only authoritative work in the field.

M H Grant's **Dictionary of British sculptors from the thirteenth to the twentieth centuries** (Rockliff, 1953) was published at the same time as Gunnis' book and covers a wider period, but it cannot be regarded as being as scholarly as the **Dictionary.** The style is very readable, but the sketches are much slighter.

Michel Seuphor's **The sculpture of this century: a dictionary of modern sculpture** (Zwemmer, 1961) gives an historic account from Rodin, at the start of this century, through the cubists, Brancusi, abstract sculpture, Gonzalez, Moore and Arp, to the present day sculpture of America and Europe. There are more than 400 illustrations and a biographical dictionary of 438 sculptors.

Parallel to **A dictionary of modern painting** by Lake and Maillard mentioned on page 33 is **A dictionary of modern sculpture** edited by Robert Maillard (Methuen, 1962). The plan is the same as that of the work on painting, and the illustrations argue eloquently the forcefulness and originality of much modern work.

Finally, a book designed primarily for the student sculptor who must acquire thorough knowledge of the materials of his art is **The materials and methods of sculpture** by Jack C Rich (OUP, 1947). There are sections on the anatomy of sculpture, plastic earths and wax, plaster of paris, on casting, the treatment of and work in metal, stone, wood and other materials, as well as an appendix of useful tables and scales and a bibliography and glossary. The book is illustrated with photographs and line drawings.

ARCHITECTURE

5 THIS CHAPTER IS almost entirely confined to books dealing with English architecture. The literature of the subject is so enormous that it would take a separate volume to analyse it all comprehensively, and to try to offer a representative coverage of the architecture of the world is impossible in the short space permitted in this book.

First of all, two sources of reference.

The British **Architects' year book** (Elek) has been published since 1945. It is concerned with articles and data on new buildings, including a technical section, and materials and equipment, with excellent illustrations and plans but no index. It has not come every year and in fact, only the eleventh volume had been published up to 1965.

From the time of the establishment of the Royal Institute of British Architects in 1834 until the publication of the **Catalogue** in 1937/8, the library of the RIBA has grown from a small collection of books, available only to London members, to one of the largest, most complete and certainly the most famous special architectural libraries in the world. Although obviously out of date this catalogue in two volumes—an author catalogue with classified and alphabetical indexes—still forms an excellent bibliography of architecture and the library, now known as the Sir Bannister Fletcher Library, issues a quarterly bulletin including an accessions list.

Historians of the subject will probably look first at two books, by Sir Bannister Fletcher and F M Simpson. Two of the most overworked words in the English language today must be ' fabulous ' and ' fantastic '. They could justifiably be used to describe **A history of architecture on the comparative method for students, craftsmen and amateurs** by Sir Bannister Fletcher. This was first published in 1896 and went into its seventeenth edition in 1961 (University of London, Athlone Press). Professor R A Cordingley of the University of Manchester was responsible for the latest revision which has brought the work fully up to date. If you want a detailed description of any important building anywhere in the world *eg* All Hallows,

London Wall, or the altar of Zeus at Pergamon, or the leaning tower of Pisa, this is the book to use. The first sixteen editions were published by Batsford, but after the author's death in 1953, the RIBA and the University of London became the joint beneficiaries of a trust fund, one of its principal assets being the copyright in this textbook. There are generous bibliographies, numerous illustrations and a full index. This is the architects' bible.

Of a more academic character, F M Simpson's **History of architectural development,** originally published early this century, is in course of republication in a new five-volume edition (Longmans, 1956; NY, McKay), four of which are already available. These cover ancient and classical architecture (Hugh Plommer), early Christian, byzantine and romanesque architecture (Cecil Stewart), gothic architecture (also Cecil Stewart), renaissance architecture (J Quentin Hughes and Norbert Lynton) and, still to come, nineteenth and twentieth century architecture (Thomas Howarth).

Richard Glazier's **Manual of historic ornament** (Batsford) reached its sixth edition in 1948. This standard work is principally useful for reference purposes and the author was an associate of the Royal Institute of British Architects and headmaster of the Municipal School of Art at Manchester, as it then was. The text is divided into two parts: the history and architecture of ornament; the application of ornament to such decorative arts as china, pottery, gold and silver, textiles, bookbinding and so on. The new edition includes Persian, Indian, Chinese and Japanese ornament. The illustrations comprise photographs and the author's own drawings but unfortunately there are no dates to the books cited in the bibliography. The book, however, is factually unique.

Everyman's concise encyclopedia of architecture (Dent; NY, Dutton) by Martin S Briggs, architect and author, was first published in 1959 and reprinted last in 1962. Here is an immense amount of information in a concise form, covering architectural terms, four hundred short biographies, styles, architectural training and bibliographical references. Numerous line drawings, done by the author himself, and photographs enhance the encyclopedia. Incidentally, Thomas Hardy gets a mention as an articled and practising architect in his early years.

You may have seen some of the cathedrals, churches and monasteries of the carolingian and romanesque periods which still stand, solid

44

and comparatively unpretentious, over most of Europe. You can learn more about the circumstances, intellectual, economic and spiritual, which produced them in Dr K J Conant's book **Carolingian and romanesque architecture 800-1200** published in 1954 by Penguin Books as an addition to the *Pelican history of art* series. Dr Conant knows the whole area concerned intimately, and has used this familiarity to paint a broad picture of the carolingian period, and the use and spread of romanesque via missionaries and colonists across Italy, Germany and France into Spain, Portugal, Hungary, Scandinavia and Britain. In the final section of the book he shows the relationship between the romanesque style and gothic, which was to follow it.

In the same series is Eberhard Hempel's **Baroque art and architecture in central Europe** (Penguin Books, 1965). The division of text is by period first, then by country, and lastly by the three ingredient subjects of architecture, sculpture and painting, although for the years 1600-1682, the three subjects came first. Architecture covers three centuries, the sixteenth to eighteenth, whilst painting and sculpture are of the seventeenth and eighteenth only. The countries dealt with are Germany, Austria, Switzerland, Hungary, Czechoslovakia and Poland.

European architecture in the twentieth century by Arnold Whittick (Crosby Lockwood, 1950/53) was originally planned as a three-volume work in five parts. Volume one, in two parts, appeared in 1950, part one dealing broadly with the main developments since the late eighteenth century to 1914, and part two with the transitional period 1919-1924. Volume two published in 1953, brings the story to 1933. Each volume has a bibliography and the indexes include references to illustrations. Buildings are treated chronologically according to dates designed or when building commenced.

The indefatigable Mrs Doreen Yarwood produced a comprehensive and detailed history of English architecture in 1963, ranging from prehistoric times to the present day. Her books, besides being authentic, always contain unexpected illustrations and this is no exception. In the **Architecture of England** (Batsford; NY, Putnam) are 1,500 drawings, many of them her own, and many more photographs, and every type of building is considered—ecclesiastical, domestic, industrial, functional and civic.

When discussing English architecture by the way, do not forget the voluminous series **The buildings of England** edited by Nikolaus

Pevsner. These are Penguin books which have been issued at intervals since 1951 on a county basis, and one of the most recent to appear and one of the most extensive in pagination is the volume on Sussex. They must be unique in format, are comprehensive in content and have illustrations and bibliographies. There are indexes of artists, and places and glossaries too. Twenty more counties are still to be covered and it is hoped that Nikolaus Pevsner will not have too much authorship trouble to enable completion to be done. The books have been described as inventories, but the information they contain make them more than that. They are paperbacks, but cloth editions have been published of certain of the volumes.

Architecture in Britain 1530-1830 (Penguin Books, fourth edition 1965) by John Summerson maintains the high standard of the *Pelican history of art* series. It gives a full account of the period, with information about important British architects, factors that influenced them and the buildings they created. The text is illustrated by numerous ground plans, and at the end of the book are 192 plates.

Henry-Russell Hitchcock wrote a two-volume authoritative work on **Early Victorian architecture in Britain** (Architectural Press, 1954) which was issued in the *Yale historical publications* series. It covers a limited period of fifteen years only, from 1837-1852 and deals with churches and chapels, country houses, palaces, banks, and other commercial buildings, houses, railway stations and the famous or infamous Crystal Palace. Volume one is a textbook of 634 pages and the second volume, though lesser in content, consists entirely of illustrations.

An introduction to English church architecture from the eleventh to the sixteenth century (OUP, 1913) is comprehensively covered by Francis Bond in this two volume work, which is intended for the great body of readers interested in medieval architecture. It is copiously illustrated, with many of the illustrations giving architectural detail. The text is subsidiary to the illustrations.

Are you interested in parish churches? If so, you could have no better guide than John Betjeman, who has done such fine programmes on this subject on British television. How they vary in size and structure and embellishment! See, for example, an illustration of the magnificent nave of St Mary Redcliffe in Bristol and alongside it, the screen and pulpit in the modest Cornish church at Blisland. The book is called **Collins guide to English parish churches**

(Collins, 1958) and more than 4,000 are described. The arrangement is by counties first and thereafter, alphabetically by town. There are 64 magnificent illustrations; drawings by John Piper; a glossary describing terms such as basilica, newel and reredos; an index of architects and artists; and an alphabetical index of places.

Who was Decimus Burton? For what buildings was he responsible? When were they erected? These are questions which H M Colvin's **Biographical dictionary of English architects 1660-1840** (Murray, 1954) will answer. Particular note should be made of the fact that it is confined to English architects and that there is a period limitation. There is an index of persons, that is people for whom properties were built and owners, and there is also an index of places.

In the same year, 1954, was published John Harvey's **English medieval architects,** a biographical dictionary down to 1550, published by the Boston Book and Art Shop USA (Batsford in UK). This also has an index under places; an index of places under countries; a chronological table of the dates of buildings from St Benet Holme Abbey in 1050 to Windsor Castle Fountain in 1558; an index under types of buildings, as abbeys, bridges, castles; and a general index— all very laudable.

Unquestionably one of the finest works on **English homes** is by Harry Avray Tipping, published by Country Life from 1921 to 1937 in nine volumes. The work is based on articles which appeared in *Country life,* the arrangement being by period and within a period, alphabetically by home.

The divisions are rather curious and there is some overlapping of dates, but broadly they run from medieval to late Georgian times.

C E C Hussey's series **English country houses** (a more appropriate title)—commenced in 1955 with the *Early Georgian* period; followed in 1956 by the *Mid-Georgian* volume and in 1958 by *Late Georgian* taking the account to 1840. These are also published by Country Life and are intended ' to narrate the architectural development of the larger country houses, to record in detail the most notable examples, to lay less stress on the biographical side and more on the architecture, and to describe more houses '.

A History of the English house from primitive times to the Victorian period was written by Nathaniel Lloyd in 1931 and reprinted by the Architectural Press in 1949. The text is arranged in centuries; the 306 pages of photographs with liberal descriptions cover exteriors, interiors, doors and doorways, windows, chimneypieces, ceilings, fireplaces, staircases and metalwork. An invaluable book, with a reliable index. 'House' is interpreted in the widest possible sense to include castles, halls and stately homes, as well as the ordinary cottage.

When it comes to visiting some of the buildings described in these books, there are a number of publications which provide information. Notable among them are **Scottish country houses and gardens open to the public** by John Fleming (1954) and **English country houses open to the public** by Christopher Hussey (1957). Both are published by Country Life. An inexpensive 'Index' publication which is revised every year is **Historic houses, castles and gardens in Great Britain and Ireland,** and the National Trust produces a variety of literature covering the properties held in its care.

If you want to know what kinds of decor were fashionable between the sixteenth and early nineteenth centuries, profitable hours may be spent with Margaret Jourdain's book **English interior decoration** (Batsford, 1950). She has divided the book into chapters on the early renaissance, the late Stuart, early Georgian, classical, regency and revived Gothic periods; and subdivided the chapters into sections on the various characteristics of the periods such as the linen-fold panelling of Tudor times, the designers who shaped them, the influence of foreign styles and so on. Where necessary, technical terms such as ' scaglia ', and ' ormolu ' are explained.

An Englishman's home is his castle. Equally, castles have been many an Englishman's home, and some castles still are. But what an aura of mystery there is about so many of these piles, now lamentably in partial decay or complete ruin. Sidney Toy has written a book about them in **The castles of Great Britain** originally published (by Heinemann) in 1953 and reissued in a third edition in 1963. Here we journey from the Roman forts, including Silchester and Portchester, to castles of the later middle ages like Naworth and Knaresborough, the latter rebuilt on the site of an older castle.

GLASS, CERAMICS AND FURNITURE

6 FIRST OF ALL, glass, which is a very specialised area of art, and one long practised in Britain, especially the ancient art of decoration with stained glass, of which more later. Specialisation is not always a blessing in the economic field, but in that of the arts the tendency of scholars ' to know more and more about less and less ' is providing us with splendid reference books on widely varying subjects, while technological advances, which frequently tend to submerge the arts in the modern world, are at least contributing to better and better illustrations for these books.

A typical reference book from the modern world is C M Elville's **Collector's dictionary of glass** (1961) published by Country Life (NY, Taplinger). Entries cover types of glass, processes of manufacture, with historical notes on glass from England and other countries, and—which is unusual—they do not halt uneasily at the beginning of the nineteenth century, but continue right up to modern times. The entries, which are quite full, are in alphabetical order and the information is supplemented by 275 photographs.

So many books in this field of the arts could be justifiably referred to as beautiful and this applies to Jaroslav R Vávra's **5,000 years of glass-making** published by Artea in Prague in 1955 (Heffer in UK). The 195 pages of text interspersed with line drawings and colour plates, are followed by 172 pages of 430 illustrations printed in blue monochrome.

Mention must be made of the excellent Victoria and Albert Museum publications on glass: **Bohemian glass** (1965) and **Glass tableware** (1947) are small booklets. **The art of glass** by Wilfred Buckley (Phaidon, 1939) is a textbook based on the Buckley collection of European glass in the museum. More extensive coverage still is W B Honey's **Glass** (Ministry of Education, 1946) a handbook for the study of glass vessels of all periods and countries, and a guide to the museum collection.

Turning now to stained glass, Bernard Rackham's **Guide to the collections of stained glass** (Board of Education, 1936) is a history

49

4

of European stained glass from the twelfth to the nineteenth centuries and has many plates in black and white, which of course, are but faint replicas of the originals. The book is based on what was then described as one of the most important museum collections in the world.

The purpose of **English stained glass** by John Baker, with excellent photographs by Alfred Lammer (Thames and Hudson, 1960; NY, Abrams) is to show why stained glass was such an important art form, to excite the interest of the reader in some of the finest works of religious art ever created, and to inform him of the development and technique of stained glass in England. There are 131 illustrations and 34 of them are in colour. The period covered is the twelfth to the sixteenth centuries.

POTTERY AND PORCELAIN

Recognised authorities with collectors, librarians, auctioneers, estate agents and dealers, valuers for probate and in the courts of law are the works by Mr William Chaffers on pottery and porcelain, and on gold and silver plate. So, at any rate, claimed an advertisement for the first edition of **The collector's handbook of marks on pottery and porcelain** in 1874. Eleven years before, Chaffers had produced his monumental **Marks and monograms on European and oriental pottery and porcelain,** now in its fifteenth edition (Reeves, 1965; USA, Borden). For the layman, however, seeking to identify a piece, reference is more easily had to a selection from Chaffers major work, entitled **The collector's handbook of marks and monograms on pottery and porcelain of the renaissance and modern periods,** in a revised and augmented edition, containing some 5,000 marks, by Frederick Litchfield (Reeves, third edition 1952).

In 1956, two leading British authorities on china marks on the staff of the Victoria and Albert Museum in London—J P Cushion and W B Honey—published a **Handbook of pottery and porcelain marks** (Faber, third edition 1965; NY, Reman). Unlike Chaffers, the arrangement here is alphabetically by country, with two sections, one for Europe, the other for China and Japan. Within a country, the various factories are listed alphabetically. The book is of value, for it includes many nineteenth and twentieth century marks not previously recorded. Line drawn maps of each country showing actual places of manufacture, are of additional interest. To each mark is appended the place-name of the factory and the name of the prin-

50

cipal proprietor where that explains the mark, the date or approximate period, and a brief description of the type of ware on which the mark is generally found. There are 444 pages of text and an index.

W B Honey has also produced a comprehensive dictionary of **European ceramic art** from the middle ages to 1815 (Faber, two volumes 1952-63). Volume one consists mainly of plates, some in colour, many more in black and white, with a brief historical summary of the period. Volume two contains details of every European pottery or porcelain manufacture of importance founded before 1815, mentioning the documentary, dated and otherwise capital pieces, and indicating the character and artistic merit of its productions so far as they have been identified. Artists and technical terms are included and there is an index to factory marks.

J P Cushion, on the other hand has written three little books which are also admirably helpful to laymen wishing to identify pieces. All are published by Faber under the title **The pocket book of [English (1959)] [German (1961)] [French and Italian (1965)] ceramic marks.** They cover the period from the sixteenth century to the present and the marks are arranged under alphabetical order of place names.

Much more detailed than these is a magnificent book for the serious collector of pottery, entitled **Encyclopedia of British pottery and porcelain marks** by Geoffrey A Godden (Herbert Jenkins, 1964; NY, Crown). The book contains more than 4,000 marks from 1650 to the present day and includes some 300 post-war studio potters, many of them recorded for the first time. The author operates a mark research and dating service for clients from all over the world, and the enquiries which he knows from experience people make have influenced the pattern of his book. Godden mentions the still unpublished list of more than 5,000 Staffordshire potters compiled by Alfred Meigh, which is now in Godden's possession.

Europe and the near east, The far east and *European porcelain* are the titles of three works by Emil Hannover which together comprise **Pottery and porcelain** (Benn, three volumes 1925). This is a learned though immensely readable treatise, which is written from the historical and artistic angle and is really intended for collectors, who are assumed already to possess a volume of pottery marks for identification purposes. There are, of course, numerous illustrations.

A very useful book for those who know what they are looking for is **Concise encyclopedia of continental pottery and porcelain** edited by R C Haggar (Deutsch, 1960). It is a most comprehensive source of reference, which took years to compile and contains information about factories, manufacturers, artists, processes, materials, potters, marks and local terminology. There are more than 400 illustrations, 24 in colour. Its companion volume is **The concise encyclopedia of English pottery and porcelain** by Mankowitz and Haggar (Deutsch, 1957).

Perhaps this author may be excused for being biased towards Frederick Litchfield, who in 1879 wrote a guide for collectors, called **Pottery and porcelain** (Black, sixth edition 1953; NY, Barrows). He lived in Hove, in Sussex, and for one man to try to cover the whole field was something of an achievement in itself. The work was completely revised in 1951 by Frank Tilley, coloured illustrations were added and new knowledge in the field of ceramics incorporated. There is a specially good chapter on counterfeit and misleading marks, although the main part of the book is taken up by descriptions of the various ceramic factories, with their marks, from Abruzzi ware to Zweibrücken, Rhenish, Bavaria. A further short chapter gives definitions of ceramic terms.

After all these scholarly works, a book intended for beginners is the **Collector's encyclopedia of English ceramics** by Bernard and Therle Hughes (Lutterworth, 1956). The beginner may like to rely on pottery marks, but the authors rightly point out that so much English china is unmarked, and much more is copied, that to develop a 'nose' for any piece is the safest and most exciting way. It is to this end that this book has been written and it follows the style of a dictionary, describing makers, patterns, styles, and places of manufacture. There are many black and white illustrations.

And finally, a book that you will enjoy reading is Bernard Hughes' **English and Scottish earthenware** (Lutterworth, 1961). It is clearly and simply written and the author's enthusiasm for the subject radiates throughout.

It traces the history of earthenware in England and Scotland from its early days through to the nineteenth century, not in enormous detail, but adequately, and it is divided, rather individually, into chapters not on pottery forms or specific periods, but into the various kinds of earthenware — tin-enamelled, transfer printed, salt-glazed

52

stoneware. This is useful if one is buying an unmarked piece of a distinct type and wants to find out its possible sources.

The art of furniture making revolves around the fact that there is comparatively little scope for creating new items of furniture, and the art is chiefly concerned with new styles and shapes of standard pieces. This is not universally true, of course, because often new technological discoveries create new products which may be employed in furnishing a house or building. Yet, in the main, furniture consists of chairs, tables, bedsteads, commodes and the familiar manufactures which western man has used in one form or another for many centuries.

Dr Hermann Schmitz **Encyclopedia of furniture** (Zwemmer, 1956; NY, Praeger) is an outline history of furniture design in near and far eastern countries, and in Europe to the mid-nineteenth century. The 53 pages of text are arranged by period and there are 320 pages of plates, from stools and bedsteads of 2000 BC (and very uncomfortable they look) to lacquer cabinets of the 1750s. Unfortunately, there is no index to text or plates.

The history of furniture and the various styles in which it has developed is illustrated in **World furniture,** edited by Helena Hayward (Hamlyn, 1965). The text consists of articles by a number of experts in particular fields; the arrangement is chronological and within the various periods by countries, Egypt, Greece and Rome to the twentieth century, and includes a bibliography and index. The book is profusely illustrated but although the colour plates are distinctively produced the details in the monochrome illustrations are not always clearly defined.

The Victoria and Albert Museum, in London, department of woodwork **Catalogue of English furniture and woodwork,** issued in four parts between 1923-1931 and covering the gothic and early Tudor periods down to the end of the Georgian, was written by H Clifford Smith (volumes one and two), Oliver Brackett (volume three) and Ralph Edwards (volume four)—all experts in their particular field. This, plus the excellent plates and bibliographies included in each volume, make these books not only a must for the serious student, but surely also an encouragement to the casual reader to pursue further a study of so fascinating a subject.

The **Dictionary of English furniture** (Country Life, revised edition in three volumes 1954) was first published in 1924-27 and was compiled by Percy Macquoid and Ralph Edwards. The vast amount of information, on eighteenth century furniture in particular, which was discovered between the wars, made a new edition essential and this was undertaken by Ralph Edwards and completed in 1954. The volumes are in alphabetical order of subject, with generous cross references, and the photographs, in chronological order, occupy 760 of the dictionary's 1,108 pages. The period covered is medieval times to 1820, and 'furniture' includes furnishings, decoration, fabrics and technical processes of decoration. It is the most important work on the subject. A shorter edition in a single volume has just been published with 684 pages and 1,900 illustrations.

What kind of fireplace was usual in an English house one thousand years ago? What is a hammerbeam roof? How did people bath, if they did, three hundred years ago? What cooking utensils were used in Georgian times? These are the kind of questions which can be answered from Doreen Yarwood's fascinating book **The English home** (Batsford, 1956; NY, Dufour) which covers interiors from Anglo-Saxon times to 1914. There are 731 illustrations and many of these are line-drawings confined to all domestic items of a particular time, made by this energetic author herself.

Four books by Margaret Jourdain which cover the years 1500-1820 in a survey of English decoration and furniture, are: **English decoration and furniture of the early renaissance: 1500-1650** (1924), **Decoration in England from 1640-1760** (written under the pseudonym Francis Lenygon—second edition 1927), **Furniture in England: 1660-1700** (also as Francis Lenygon—second edition 1924) and **English decoration and furniture of the later eighteenth century: 1760-1820** (1922). All the books are published by Batsford.

Another useful catalogue is that of the **Wallace collection** in London, which was compiled by F J B Watson in 1956. Most of it deals with French furniture—gothic to nineteenth century—and there are a few references to English and Italian work. Each piece is described in detail with full documentation.

So far, we have described substantial or encyclopedic works on furniture. In 1952, John Gloag produced **A short dictionary of furniture** (Allen and Unwin) containing 1,764 terms used in Great Britain and America. Preliminary chapters to the dictionary itself are concerned with the description and design of furniture, whilst subsidiary chapters give a short list of British and American furniture makers and designers, and British clock makers (this being very sketchy); a short list of books and periodicals on the subject; tables by countries, from Saxon times, of the types of furniture made, the methods of construction, the materials used, the makers and styles and fashions. There are 630 illustrations.

A most interesting volume is Sir Ambrose Heal's **London furniture makers: 1680-1840** (Batsford, 1953) which contains attractive reproductions of the original trade cards of many makers, in a list of some 2,500, painstakingly compiled from old directories and trade cards. This is a specialist volume intended for collectors, but nonetheless fascinating for that.

Two books by Clifford Musgrave, director of the Royal Pavilion at Brighton, must be mentioned. **Regency furniture 1800-1830** (Faber, 1961) is an exact and penetrating stylistic analysis with 137 illustrations, nineteen of them of furniture in the Pavilion itself. The period was an age of elegance, with restraint on the one hand and florid, classical decoration on the other. French and Chinese influences are closely examined; then comes an equally close study of different types of furniture, processes and materials, and there is a list of the principal cabinet-making woods and a glossary of unusual terms. A full bibliography and a workable index complete a fine book. **Adam and Hepplewhite and other neo-classical furniture** (Faber, 1966) is an excellent reference book, revealing painstaking research and being a guide to many stately homes. Robert Adam, architect and designer, after a grand tour and a long stay in Europe at the time of new discoveries at Herculaneum and Pompeii, absorbed the styles of the new motifs and embarked on remodelling and designing great country and large town houses. The very fine photographs here—177 of them—show the wide range of neoclassical styles in furniture up to the year 1790 and there are many of Adam's drawings. Biographical details are given of Adam, Hepplewhite and their contemporaries, and details too, of the materials and processes used.

Finally, an odd corner of furniture making. **English lookingglasses** by Geoffrey Wills (Country Life, 1965) is a study of glass, frames and makers in the period 1670-1820. This is a unique and beautifully produced monograph, which includes 164 plates and also has a directory of London makers and sellers of looking glasses. It is abundantly clear from the illustrations how patience and craftsmanship went hand in hand in those days.

SOME MISCELLANEA

7 THE SUBJECTS COVERED in this chapter are: engraving, metals and jewellery, coins and tokens, clocks and watches. The first three all involve work with metal or stones, the last named subject is one which is more often described, in the world of antiques, as ' automata '.

ENGRAVING

One of the standard works on the history of engraving and etching is by a former Oxford University professor of fine art, Arthur M Hind. It is called **A history of engraving and etching from the fifteenth century to 1915** (Constable, third edition 1923; Gloucester, Massachusetts, Peter Smith). Eight chapters deal with the history of the art and a ninth describes the tone processes of mezzotint, crayon, stipple, aquatint and colour-prints; the tenth chapter deals with modern etchers and their methods. There is an exhaustive bibliography and classified lists of engravers.

Another work of formidable scholarship by the same author is **Engraving in England in the sixteenth and seventeenth centuries** (CUP, three volumes 1952-64). They are described in A J Walford's *Guide to reference material* as representing ' The most complete work of its kind with the fullest possible information about every known work of the engravers mentioned '.

Professor Hind also set out to write a detailed general history of the art of woodcutting, but this was never completed.

In the first of the two finished volumes (both published by Constable; Gloucester, Massachusetts, Peter Smith), entitled **An introduction to a history of woodcut** he examines processes and materials, gives a general historical survey of woodcuts from the fifteenth to the twentieth century and then considers single cuts before the period of book illustration. Volume two deals with European book illustrations and single cuts in the fifteenth century. Chapters on the various countries are broken down into sections on towns where the most famous painters and artists of the fifteenth century worked.

The subject is considered from both the technical and artistic standpoints. There are profuse footnotes on every page, frequent illustrations and a bibliography at the end of every chapter. Not a work for general reading, these two volumes are a remarkable source of factual information on the fifteenth century, gleaned by the author from one of the largest print collections in the world.

Professor Hind was content just to write the preface to **German engravings, etchings and woodcuts 1400-1700** by F W H Hollstein (Amsterdam, Herzberger, seven volumes 1950-64). In his preface he remarks that the author has embarked on one of the most ambitious undertakings in the whole record of iconography. A total of some twenty volumes is planned, but publication proceeds now without the original author who died recently. The arrangement is alphabetical by engraver and the finished work will contain 8,000 important prints, more than half of which have never been published before. Hollstein also commenced the publication (in 1949) of **Dutch and Flemish etchings, engravings and woodcuts 1450-1700** (Zwemmer), fifteen volumes out of a projected twenty five having so far appeared.

The term etching has been applied in so many different and often incorrect ways that a definition is now fundamental to any modern work. Colonel Maurice H. Grant, in an excellent introduction to **A dictionary of British etchers** (Rockliff, 1952), compares the types and method used with those of allied reproduction arts. He discusses the various schools and historical backgrounds, and gives other notes most valuable to the collector. The dictionary itself mentions dates, where obtainable, details of exhibitions and the best known work of each artist.

Engravings and their value by J Herbert Slater (Link House, sixth edition 1929) is described as a complete guide to the collection and prices of all classes of prints, with more than 300 reproductions. For current prices, the work is obviously out of date, but as a guide to the art of engraving—in wood, in stipple, to etching, mezzotints, aquatints, proofs, states, forgeries and so on, and for accounts of engravers and their works, it is still unsurpassed. It covers artists in the field until about 1900. Walter Sickert, for example, has only a couple of lines with one attribution.

The six-volume **Catalogue of seals in the department of manuscripts in the British Museum** compiled by W de G Birch (1887-1900) is worth mentioning at this point. The collection is most comprehensive and presents a fascinating variety of artistic design in a practical area of art which has now lost much of its former commercial importance.

METALS AND JEWELLERY

This is a fascinating and popular field of art in which, by the nature of its creations, interest remains as strong today as it has ever been, and the aesthetic values of twentieth century design are being harmoniously applied to precious metal and stones with all the elegance and enthusiasm of the old craftsmen.

But when considering older work, C A Markham's revision of Chaffer's **Handbook to hallmarks on gold and silver plate** (Reeves, eighth edition 1961; USA, Borden) is a valuable aid to identifying and dating early specimens.

Bernard and Therle Hughes, a well-known combination in the artistic field, have compiled a book **Three centuries of English domestic silver 1500-1820** which was published by Lutterworth in 1952. Cardinal Wolsey, we read, ' entertained important guests and all their hundreds of gentleman followers with banquets served on gold and silver dishes to a total of thirty bullock wagon loads '. In the sixteenth century, silver was the possession of the wealthy few. Later in the period covered, it was to enter the houses of humbler folk. After a first chapter on hallmarks, twenty one other chapters deal with different categories of silverware. Each is described in a chatty way against the social background. Illustrations are numerous, in line and half tone, and there is a good index.

Another useful book on old silver is by Seymour B Wyler, **Book of old silver: English-American-foreign** (NY, Crown, eleventh edition 1949). After introductory chapters on the legal history, frauds, the collecting and care of old silver, different items are discussed, such as tableware, lighting appliances, boxes and so on. Then come tables of hallmarks on English, Scottish and Irish plate; Sheffield plate; and the marks used by American, French, German and other silversmiths. There is a short bibliography and a number of good half tone plates.

Unquestionably one of the most lavishly produced books in the artistic field is Sir Charles James Jackson's **Illustrated history of English plate, ecclesiastical and secular** (Country Life, two volumes 1911). This takes up the story in 1500 BC. There are two lists of illustrations, one of those in photogravure, and the other a chronological list of all the objects illustrated. Incidentally, the author makes it clear that his term 'plate' includes gold, silver and baser metals sometimes overlaid with gold.

Two important books of reference are Sir Charles James Jackson's **English goldsmiths and their marks** (Batsford, second edition 1949; NY, Dover) and **The London goldsmiths 1200-1800** by Sir Ambrose Heal (CUP, 1935). Jackson's book contains more than 13,000 marks reproduced in facsimile from authentic examples of plate, and tables of date-letters and other hallmarks used in the UK assay offices. The coverage includes silversmiths. Heal's book is intended to complement the other work, by providing a record of the names and addresses of the craftsmen, their shop signs and trade cards. The book shows where a man's place of business was, what sign he used and when and where he moved. The Jackson book establishes the identity and date of a piece from its mark.

Howard Herschel Cotterell deals with **Old pewter: its makers and marks in England, Scotland and Ireland** (Batsford, 1929; Rutland, Vermont, Tuttle). The author is an acknowledged expert on his subject, and his book illustrates all known marks and secondary marks of the old pewterers, and has a series of plates showing their principal wares. All the marks illustrated were drawn by the author from originals or from rubbings. Pewter used, of course, to be the main material from which common domestic utensils were made. It is an alloy of tin and lead.

Even more enticing than gold and silver work is jewellery.

Jewels were always meant to be worn and handled to bring them to life and afford the owner the greatest satisfaction and pleasure. Whilst we are grateful that so many beautiful examples of this art through the ages are now preserved in museums, their incarceration behind glass deprives us of part of their joy. Many wonderful jewels are described and finely illustrated in **A history of jewellery 1100-1870** by Joan Evans (Faber, 1953). There is a good index and an extensive bibliography.

R M Shipley's **Dictionary of gems and gemology** (Los Angeles, Gemological Institute of America, fifth edition 1951) on the other hand, is a glossary of more than 40,000 English and foreign words, terms and abbreviations to be found in English literature in connection with gems and jewellery, and artistic subjects in general. The most recent edition contains added material on synthetic stones.

Brief histories of many famous jewels will be found and much data is essentially mineralogic.

Another book for those who like to feast their eyes on the riches of the world is E F Twining (Baron Twining of Tanganyika) **A history of the crown jewels of Europe** (Batsford, 1960; NY, London House). This is a sumptuous volume with more than 200 fine photographs and a most detailed text, arranged by country, in which the wealth of information is (comparatively speaking) equal to that of the treasures described.

One of the most popular books on the subject, for many reasons, not least its appearance in library catalogues but its disappearance from the shelves, is Arnold Selwyn's **Retail jeweller's handbook and merchandise manual for sales personnel** (Heywood). Originally published in 1945, it reached its seventh edition in 1962. This is a prescribed textbook for the UK retail jeweller's diploma course and has now been thoroughly revised and brought up to date by G F Andrews and J J Adler. To know the characteristics, properties and limitations of the articles sold is essential in the jeweller's business above all others, say the revisers in their introduction. There are many illustrations, including some beautiful colour plates of gemstones in their natural and cut states, supplied by the British Museum. An appendix gives various tables of weight, specific gravities and melting points of various metals.

Lastly, a visual delight is **The art of Carl Fabergé** by A Kenneth Snowman (Faber, third edition 1964; NY, Tudor). It is packed with the most beautiful illustrations of the master's work, many of them in colour, and besides the exhaustive provenances of individual items, has a chronological table of events in Fabergé's life.

COINS AND TOKENS

How often have you come across a coin which defied identification? Or are you one of those lucky, or unlucky individuals who is landed with a heterogeneous collection of coins, probably through the death of a relative, and wonder if there is anything of value! For identification, the fifty two volumes issued by the **Department of coins and medals of the British Museum** since 1873 are unquestionably the best source of reference. These volumes are monuments of scholarship and each consists of an historical survey, a bibliography, a catalogue arranged by mints and illustrations. They cover: the gold and silver coins of the ancients—700 BC to AD 1; Chinese coins from the seventh century BC to AD 21; Persian, Greek, Indian and imperial byzantine coins; coins of the Roman empire; of the Vandals, Ostrogoths and Lombards, and most interesting of all to us, the coins of Great Britain and Ireland. Obviously, only the largest libraries will have all these volumes—there are twenty nine describing the coins of Greece alone.

Coins of the world of the nineteenth and twentieth centuries, to 1954 in fact, are dealt with by W Raymond in two volumes published in New York by Wayte Raymond (Bailey Bros in UK), but **English coins from the seventh century to 1950** were described by G C Brooke in a book last revised in 1955 (Methuen, third edition; NY, Humanities Press). This is very useful for identification as there are many plates, but once a coin is identified, the next question is, how much is it worth? For British and Irish coins, the well-known London firm of Seaby publish a standard catalogue which lists coins from 100 BC to date. If you use this catalogue, remember that the prices given are for coins in fine condition and the buying-in price will obviously be less.

What is hogmoney? Or binericle money? Is there an elephant coin? Or a brass farthing? These questions and dozens more can be answered by the **Teach yourself guide to numismatics:** an ABC of coin collecting, compiled by C C Chamberlain (EUP, 1960), in the well-known *Teach yourself* series. It is, in fact, a dictionary of coins and deals with coinage in the widest sense, even including window tax. Why were houses with six windows or more subject to a tax in 1695? To defray the enormous expense of the great recoinage that became necessary owing to the clipping and defacing of the old hammered coinage. And the tax was not repealed until 1851! A very useful pocket-book of facts with many illustrations.

William Boyne wrote his book on **Seventeenth century trade tokens** in 1858. Fresh information came to light every year thereafter, errors were rectified and a new edition prepared by George Williamson in two volumes in 1889. It is a sine qua non for the collector of tokens, and a valuable book of reference for compilers of family records and pedigrees, workers in folklore, local antiquarians and county archaeologists. Tokens were issued in England, Wales and Ireland from 1648 to 1679 and were the small change of the period of the small trader and local authorities. They usually bear on the obverse the name of the issuer and on the reverse, the place of issue. The arrangement of the book is by county and within county, alphabetical by place. There are twelve indexes to the voluminous information under such headings as places, shapes, values, christian and surnames of issuers and armorial bearings.

Perhaps librarians and museum curators should know best of all how difficult it is to identify coins and they would doubtless say that of all those produced, eighteenth century tokens are most in evidence today. For help in this direction, therefore, R Dalton and S H Hamer's **Provincial token coinage of the eighteenth century** (Spink, three volumes 1910-15) is the most valuable book of reference; this follows on where Boyne leaves off. Volumes one and two deal with English counties, volume three with Wales, Scotland and Ireland. The arrangement is alphabetical by county and notes are given of rarity. Illustrations are plentiful. There is a supplement by A W Waters **Notes on eighteenth century tokens** (Seaby, 1954) which expands some of the information in the parent work.

CLOCKS AND WATCHES

When antique clocks are mentioned, one immediately thinks of Thomas Tompion whose timepieces today fetch incredibly high prices in the salerooms. It is hard to credit that there have been 35,000 makers of clocks and watches in the world and they are listed in two books, F J Britten's **Old clocks and watches and their makers** (Spon, seventh edition 1956) and G H Baillie's **Watchmakers and clockmakers of the world** (NAG Press, third edition 1951). Look for the maker's name on the face of your timepiece or behind the works, and you will be able to discover where the maker operated and when.

Britten lists 14,000 makers in alphabetical order. The book was first published in 1899 and contains historical and descriptive accounts of the different styles of English and foreign clocks and watches, with many excellent illustrations.

Baillie's book is a list of makers, and also has a list of place names with references to maps, English and European. Initials and monograms can also be identified.

Britten also compiled a dictionary and guide book in 1878 called **Watch and clock makers' handbook** (Spon; Princeton, Van Nostrand) which reached its fifteenth edition in 1955. It will answer questions about the calendar clock, the verge movement and what a ' throw ' is.

A more recent encyclopedia still is Donald de Carle's **Watch and clock encyclopedia** (NAG Press, second edition 1959). This is a more compact dictionary than Britten's and more popularly presented. Ernst von Bassermann-Jordan's **Book of old clocks and watches** (Allen and Unwin, 1964) has long been regarded as a standard textbook for connoisseurs and collectors. It was originally published in Germany as *Uhrem,* but a fourth revised edition was translated into English for the first time in 1964. There are some beautiful illustrations, many of them in colour, and this is the most up to date book on this fascinating subject, covering time-measuring instruments of 3,000 years ago, as well as clocks and watches.

COSTUME AND STAGE DESIGN

8 COSTUME IS ONE of the most colourful and charming of all the arts. It is also, of course, a subject of considerable historical and social importance, in the manner in which it illustrates dress and customs through the ages.

There are two principal bibliographies: René Colas **Bibliographie generale du costume et de la mode** published in two volumes by the author in Paris in 1933 (NY, Hacker) and **Bibliography of costume** by Hilaire and Meyer Hiler (NY, H W Wilson Co, 1939). The first of these is an alphabetical arrangement by author, title and series of books and periodicals in all languages concerned with civil, military and ecclesiastical dress, as well as millinery, fashion, hair styles and accessories. The Hiler bibliography is nearly three times the size of Colas' work and takes the form of a dictionary catalogue, including not only works on costume but also books on other subjects which discuss or illustrate costume. The bibliography was based on the authors' catalogue of their own personal library, published in 1927.

Two other reference works which may be useful are **Costume index** by Isabel Stevenson Monro and Dorothy E Cook (NY, H W Wilson Co, 1937), and C H Gibbs-Smith's book, also entitled **Costume index** but unpublished, which is kept at the Victoria and Albert Museum in London in manuscript, and is an index to material in the museum's collection; it was compiled in 1936 and although valuable and unique, has not been kept up to date. The American work is in two volumes and provides an extensive guide to plates or illustrated text in nearly 1,000 titles covering the whole range of costume.

Turning now to specific accounts, a specialised volume is **Peasant costume in Europe** by Kathleen Mann (Black, 1950) originally published in two volumes in 1931 and 1936. It is sad that we English have no traditional national dress, but here are accounts of costumes made by peasants from materials woven by themselves and embroidered with their own designs. These dresses were often worn only on special occasions and have been handed down by successive generations.

Mary G Houston has compiled fascinating books on **Ancient Egyptian, Mesopotamian and Persian costume and decoration** (Black, second edition 1954; NY, Barnes & Noble); **Ancient Greek, Roman and Byzantine costume** (Black, second edition 1963; NY, Barnes & Noble); and **Medieval costume in England and France** (Black, 1939; NY, Barnes & Noble). The author stresses that the construction of each costume has been studied and each type cut out, draped or made up before being sketched. There are fine illustrations and a bibliography which surprises by the number of books published on these ancient themes.

Another comprehensive work for art student, illustrator, theatrical designer and fashion artist, as well as for the general reader, is Angela Bradshaw's **World costumes** (NY, Macmillan, 1959). There are 142 pages of outstanding drawings, with brief and adequate notes to describe the origin and evolution of costume of all ages and all countries.

Had it been possible for Herbert Norris to complete his **Costume and fashion: the evolution of European dress through the earliest ages** it would certainly have been one of the most ambitious and comprehensive surveys of costume, mainly British, through the ages. Volumes one, two, three and six were published by Dent (NY, Dutton) between 1924 and 1938, covering the earliest ages down to the end of the Tudors, and the nineteenth century. Stuart and Hanoverian times were to have been dealt with in the unpublished fourth and fifth volumes. The numerous illustrations in black and white, including patterns, are taken from line drawings, with additional colour reproductions from somewhat stylised paintings.

The county libraries section of the UK Library Association published a **Guide to books on costume** in their *Reader's guide* series in 1961. This is a selective list which does not carry many annotations and which excludes books in foreign languages, but theatrical costume is specially dealt with.

Nevil Truman's **Historic costuming** (Pitman, 1936) is intended for theatrical producers and designers, both professional and amateur. The story begins with the Greeks in 550 BC and proceeds, chiefly through the English scene, to 1910. Dress of the clergy and fashions in armour receive special attention in the three final

65

5

chapters, and there is an appendix of diagrams showing the evolution of styles. A feature of the book is the large number of excellent illustrations, many of them in colour.

Doreen Yarwood in **English costume from the second century BC to 1960** (Batsford, second edition 1961; NY, Dufour) has provided in one volume a fairly comprehensive survey of dress in England from the earliest times to the present day, with introductory chapters on the ancient civilisations in order to trace the origins of our own costume. Bibliographies guide the student to sources of more detailed knowledge and the book is exceptionally well illustrated by line drawings in black and white and attractive colour plates selected from contemporary illustrations of the periods concerned.

The man and wife team of Doctor Cecil Willett Cunnington and Phyllis Cunnington have compiled five handbooks of **English costume: medieval** (1952); **sixteenth century** (1956); **seventeenth century** (1955); **eighteenth century** (second edition 1965); **nineteenth century** (1959); all published by Faber (NY, Dufour). These are designed principally for producers of stage and screen, but contain many interesting sidelights which will entertain the historically minded as well.

Contemporaneously with these, the Cunningtons were compiling a concise reference dictionary of English costume which must have grown apace as their researches proceeded. This they proposed to publish, but it so happened that Charles Beard had also been collecting material for an encyclopedic work on English costume. His interest was in the early centuries, and at his death, the Cunningtons were glad to have his material to add to their own. The result is **A dictionary of English costume from 900-1900** (Black, 1960).

Historical costumes of England from the eleventh to the twentieth century (Harrap, second edition 1958) are discussed in thirty six sections by Nancy Bradfield, roughly corresponding to the reigns of British sovereigns. The illustrations in the second edition are entirely new and there are hundreds of them taken from contemporary sources, with a commentary on the facing page.

National costume has always attracted great interest, particularly perhaps from those whose own national heritage does not include such colourful dress. Max Tilke's **Oriental costumes: their designs and colours** and **The costumes of eastern Europe,** published in Berlin by Ernst Wasmuth in 1922 and 1925, and **A pictorial history**

of costume, written in collaboration with Wolfgang Bruhn and published in England by Zwemmer in 1955 (NY, Praeger) form a valuable contribution to the study of this field. All three contain colour plates and are excellently illustrated, showing both complete costumes and details of individual garments. Monochrome and colour plates, with descriptive notes, also make up the author's survey of costume patterns and designs of all periods and nations from antiquity to modern times, published in this country in 1956 by Zwemmer (NY, Praeger) under the title **Costume patterns and designs.**

The rich colouring of Italian costume is finely illustrated in the colour plates which form the major part of **Il costume popolare in Italia** by Emma Calderini, published in 1946 by Sperling and Kupfer of Milan in a limited edition. The Italian text consists of a general introduction to the costume of the country followed by descriptive notes to the plates, which are arranged geographically to illustrate the dress in the various provinces of Italy.

Another earlier publication, still valuable for the clarity of the illustrations, is **The costumes of all nations from the earliest times to the nineteenth century** by Albert Kretschmer and Carl Rohrbach, issued by Henry Sotheran in 1882. This consists of a series of colour plates, arranged chronologically and then by country but only with titles to the figures shown and no descriptive notes.

Change in fashion always corresponds with outlook. Dissatisfaction with one has always implied a similar criticism of the other. In the early part of the nineteenth century the apparent state of arrest in the feminine outlook was followed by the same lack of change in fashion. The changing social scene of the latter half of the century was soon reflected in the costume of the period. Doctor Cecil Willett Cunnington's study of **English women's clothing in the nineteenth century** (Faber, 1937) makes this point obvious. The book contains a wealth of descriptive detail and is profusely illustrated with reproductions of contemporary fashion plates, line drawings and colour photographs of examples from the author's collection of costume. This is a fascinating study of an era in which fashion decreed that woman's shape should be anything but that of her natural form! Anne Buck's **Victorian costume and costume accessories** (Jenkins, 1961) gives a further detailed study of this period.

The theory that change in fashion illustrates mass psychology and this forms an important part of social history is further substantiated by a study of contemporary (up to 1950) styles in Cunnington's **English women's clothing in the present century** (Faber, 1952).

Reproductions in colour from portraits of children by the great masters form the illustrations to Percy MacQuoid **Four hundred years of children's costume** covering 1400-1800, issued by the Medici Society in 1923. Descriptive notes accompany each plate and, as only the aristocracy could afford to have their children painted, the costume depicted is inevitably that of the young people of the well-to-do families of the time.

Reproductions from contemporary sources, in monochrome and colour, also illustrate the six parts which form volume three of a series edited by James Laver entitled **Costume of the western world.** These were issued in 1951 by Harrap and no further titles have appeared to date. Fashion in England, France, Holland and Spain during 1485-1625 is described by experts and short bibliographies are included in each book.

Particularly valuable for details of the medieval and renaissance periods is James Robinson Planché's **A cyclopedia of costume; or, dictionary of dress,** published in two volumes by Chatto and Windus, 1876-79. Volume one is a dictionary of costume and volume two a history of costume in Europe from the commencement of the Christian era to the accession of George the third. Numerous illustrations include some colour plates.

An unusual, interesting and helpful book for the subject of costume is Vyvyan Holland's **Hand coloured fashion plates 1770-1899** (Batsford, 1955), a study of their origin, evolution and decline. The author in his introduction says that without the existence of these plates it would be almost impossible to study the evolution of costume at all. He defines a fashion plate as a drawing made for the purpose of showing people the right kind of clothes for them to wear to be abreast of the fashion of the moment, and a means of predicting what the fashionable person will be wearing in the near future. Most of the plates are reproduced in black and white, the earliest being of 1654, although the title gives the commencement date as 1770. In fact, there are six seventeenth century engravings.

68

All the 685 illustrations of historic costume in Henry Harald Hansen's **Costume cavalcade** are in colour. The book was first published in Copenhagen in 1954, but came in an English edition from Methuen in 1956. The arrangement is chronological, from 3,000 BC to the twentieth century, and there are lists of sources and of a few books on costumes.

A thousand years of dress are covered by Henry Shaw in **Dresses and decorations of the middle ages from the seventh to the seventeenth centuries** (William Pickering, 1843) in two volumes. Emphasis should be placed on the decorations in this scholarly work with its extensive historical detail from original manuscript sources, for they include such items as King Alfred's jewel, mitres, chasubles and reliquaries.

Mary Evans' **Costume throughout the ages** (Lippincott, revised edition 1950) has many black and white illustrations and the book deals with historic dress of the ancients to 1950, and with national costume.

By modern standards, the colour plates in Adolf Rosenberg's **Design and development of costume from prehistoric times up to the twentieth century** published in five volumes by Foyles in 1925, are not well defined. Nevertheless, this exhaustive series of plates forms a most valuable reference source, necessitating the use of the index.

Finally, a note of four rather specialised books. Talbot Hughes **Dress design: an account of costume for artists and dressmakers** (Pitman, 1926) is a history of English costume which also gives technical patterns from which single items of apparel can be made up. Dr Cunnington and his wife have written **History of underclothes** (Joseph, 1951). We cannot appreciate the outer garment, they say, unless we understand the nature of the supporting garments beneath, and this book attempts to do just that for English underclothes worn by both sexes from 1485. Florence Anslow's **Practical millinery** (Pitman, 1922), although dated, has a short account of the history of head-wear, followed by detailed instructions on how to make head-gear of all shapes and sizes. Whereas Florence Anslow's book is mainly for those who make hats, Michael Harrison's **History of the hat** (Jenkins, 1960) is an historical account from Etruscan influences and basic forms, to the trilby, the bowler and the 'Anthony Eden'. As is obvious, therefore, it deals with styles and types of all countries, is well illustrated with small marginal drawings, and has a list source material.

This branch of costume has a special fascination, which is well brought out in Major R M Barnes' book **A history of the regiments and uniforms of the British army** (Seeley Service Co). The account covers the years from 1642-1915 and there are a number of colour plates.

In progress is Cecil C P Lawson's **History of the uniforms of the British army** from the beginnings to 1760, of which four volumes of the projected five have been published so far. Volumes one and two were published by Peter Davies in 1940/41 and volumes three and four by Norman Military Publications in 1961 and 1966. The illustrations are all in black and white.

A very recent publication is Karel Toman's **Book of military uniforms and weapons:** *an illustrated survey of military dress, arms and practice through the ages* (Hamlyn, 1964). Neither a scientific study nor a detailed survey of the history of warfare, this book is content to give a broad outline of the appearance of warriors in bygone times and trace the changes that have occurred in costume and manner of fighting. The illustrations, in line drawings in black and white and colour, are numerous but not particularly clearly defined.

The National Maritime Museum sponsored **The dress of the British sailor,** compiled by Sir Gerald Dickens (HMSO, 1957). Although consisting only of eight pages of text and 24 plates, this gives an excellent picture of sailors' dress from the fourteenth century to the present day and includes the badges and specialisation letters of the ranks of the present day navy. More specific still is John Mollo's **Uniforms of the royal navy during the Napoleonic wars** (Hugh Evelyn, 1965). Intended for the student as much as the general reader, this book, albeit of awkward format, is beautifully illustrated by silhouette form plates (a popular style of portraiture of the time) from contemporary sources.

COSTUME AND STAGE DESIGN
Certain books concerned with costume have been written primarily with the idea of theatrical productions, and one of the most recent is Fairfax Proudfit Walkup's **Dressing the part:** *a history of costume*

for the theatre (Owen, 1959; NY, Appleton). From early Egyptian times to the present, costume is described in chapters which each deal with a specific period. The history of the period is followed by an account of the costume development, then detailed descriptions of the dress, undergarment and accessories. For practical purposes, there are sketches and easy-to-follow patterns, with directions on how to make the various garments. Particularly useful too, is the selected list of period plays from Egyptian times until now, with a full bibliography of books and periodicals and 328 illustrations.

Mary Fernald and Eileen Shenton's **Costume design and making: a practical handbook** (Black, 1958; NY, Dufour) is a book for all who are interested in historical dress, and for those who wish to make and design costumes for the stage, pageants and fancy-dress balls. There are pattern diagrams of English costume from Saxon times to the late Victorian era, and detailed notes are given for the making of the costumes, their colours and textures. Stage lighting and its effects are also considered.

Dressing the play is a *How to do it book* (Studio Vista, 1953) by Norah Lambourne, staff tutor with the British Drama League on stagecraft in schools and colleges, and by dramatic societies. Jewellery and accessories are specially dealt with, as is the use of fabrics and surface décor. There is a bibliography and a very short list of materials stockists.

James Laver's **Costume in the theatre** (Harrap, 1964) ranges over the centuries from Greek drama to the present century, and takes in opera and ballet. The many illustrations are drawn from playbills, posters, drawings of old masters and engravings as might be expected from the former keeper of prints and drawings at the Victoria and Albert Museum.

On the other hand, Margot Lister's **Stage Costume** (Jenkins, 1954) is a small practical handbook. In a mere 96 pages, dress is considered from Egyptian times to 1900 and there are clear and expressive drawings. As an actress and producer herself, she has been able to interpret the practical requirements of the stage.

Costumes for schoolplays by Barbara Snook (Batsford, 1965) is the result of twenty years' experience of designing and making costumes and properties in a girls' grammar school. Amateur societies will also benefit from these practical suggestions which cover dyeing, armour, accessories, make-up, masks, and properties in addition to the costume itself. There are many very expressive line drawings with clues on how to make various dress and auxiliary items from medieval times to the eighteenth century. On the same subject is A V White's **Making stage costumes for amateurs** (Routledge, 1957). Here are instructions on how to form the basic wardrobe and there is a chapter on costume for folk dancing. There are a few line drawings, not as comprehensive as those in Barbara Snook's book.

Period costumes and settings for the small stage by Joyce M Conyngham Green (Harrap, 1936) covers English costuming from William the Conqueror to the regency period and has some useful tips, but the presentation of ideas has been bettered in the more recent books already quoted. Ken Etheridge, producer for the Cymric Players, produced a small book on **Stage costume for the amateur** from Greek times to the nineteenth century (Edinburgh, Albyn Press, 1942) which, though brief, is essentially practical.

One of the most recent books, and a unique one too, is **Stage design throughout the world since 1950,** edited by René Hainaux, chief editor of World Theatre, and Yves-Bonnat (Harrap, 1964; NY, Theatre Arts). It has been compiled with the help of the International Theatre Institute and is essentially a pictorial record. In fact, the production is sumptuous and publication was under the patronage of UNESCO. It is a companion volume to **Stage design throughout the world since 1935** (Harrap, new edition 1966) and presents fifteen countries not included in the first book, including India, Spain and USSR. There are more than 500 illustrations, grouped in alphabetical order of country, and there is a list of stage designers, giving biographical notes on over 300 of them. Materials, equipment and lighting are discussed and the two books give a very exhaustive account of modern stage techniques and equipment.

A specialised book is **Historic hairdressing** by Joyce Asser (Pitman, 1966), a lecturer at Tottenham Technical College. Here are hair styles from Assyrian times to the present day. It is directed towards designers working in the theatre, and television and costume designers. There are many line drawings, which help immensely.

To end this chapter, a glance at four books of national interest to British readers, for whom the tartans of the Scottish clans represent perhaps the most picturesque substitute for a truly national costume.

One of the most comprehensive works on tartans is Robert Bain's **The clans and tartans of Scotland** (Collins, fourth edition 1959). Arranged alphabetically by clan it gives a brief history of each. Tartans are illustrated in colour, together with a drawing and description of the clansmen's crest, the motto and the origin and gaelic version of the name of each clan.

The Scottish tartans illustrated by William Semple (Edinburgh, Johnston, second edition 1959) also gives historical sketches of the clans and families of Scotland, with badges and arms of the chiefs and their families; and the various traditional setts are well defined and illustrated in Donald Calder Stewart's study of **The setts of the Scottish tartans with descriptive and historical notes** (Oliver and Boyd, 1950) which includes a bibliography and diagrams of all the setts discussed.

Finally, **Scottish costume 1550-1850** by Stuart Maxwell and Robin Hutchison (NY, Dufour) has been compiled from original sources, from costumes themselves, from portraits and sculpture, from memoirs and travel books and from accounts of the buying of costume found in official and private records. Chapters are also devoted to Highland dress and especially its later development, to jewellery and weapons.

CRAFTS

9 BY DEFINITION IT may seem paradoxical to include a chapter entitled ' crafts ' in a book about fine arts, but there are one or two topics which it would be a pity to miss out just because they do not, technically, count as arts.

First of all, a general title, **Handbook of crafts** edited by Griselda Lewis (Studio Vista, 1960) is full of practical instructions on hooking rings, framing pictures, making shell pictures, toys, puppets, jewellery and a host of other things which can be made without specialised or expensive equipment.

C E C Tattersall's **A history of British carpets from the introduction of the craft until the present day** (Lewis, 1933) is a chronological survey of the art of handmade carpets in Great Britain, from the sixteenth to the twentieth centuries, including turkey work, hand-knotted and embroidered examples, with a final section on machine-made carpets and their manufactures. Finely illustrated by photographic plates, some in colour, there are many reproductions of examples from the department of textiles in the Victoria and Albert Museum, to the staff of which the author was attached when this book was written.

Barbara Snook's **English historical embroidery** (Batsford, 1960) is arranged chronologically and within each period, subdivided to show the types of embroidery typical of the time. The book is well illustrated in black and white and includes an index and a bibliography citing particularly publications of the Victoria and Albert Museum. A useful book, not only for the student of the embroiderer's art, but for those interested in the history of costume.

The craft of the smith is described by John Starkie Gardner in **English ironwork of the seventeenth and eighteenth centuries** (Batsford, 1911) which the author calls an historical and analytical account. Firebacks will not be found here, as the author confined himself to exterior ironwork, including gates, railings, balustrades, balconies, stair ramps, grilles, lampholders, brackets, signs and vanes. There is an alphabetical list of smiths, architects and designers, and also an alphabetical list of illustrations under place.

Much more recent are Raymond Lister's **Decorative cast ironwork in Great Britain** (Bell, 1960) and **Decorative wrought ironwork in Great Britain** (Bell, 1957). The author, Raymond Lister, is the third generation to run the family business (Architectural Metalwork Ltd) at Cambridge, and he deals with architectural and domestic ironwork in both books. In the former he also discusses the foundry worker, and in the latter, the blacksmith, alas now a dying craft. There are glossaries of terms used in the industry in both volumes and extensive bibliographies. There are magnificent line drawings and half-tone illustrations, and the books are more comprehensive than Gardner, dealing with interior and domestic appliances as well as exterior examples of the smith's craftsmanship.

Pieter van den Bosch painted a tranquil and colourful study of *The lace maker,* which is a famous reminder of one of the old domestic crafts. In Gertrude Whiting's **A lace guide for makers and collectors** (NY, Dutton, 1920) there are suggestions for making lace, rules for making (very detailed and attractive, this) and an extensive five-language vocabulary of special terms.

Mary Symonds and Louisa Preece are the joint authors of **Needlework through the ages** (Hodder, 1928) which is beautifully illustrated with fine photographs chronologically arranged to give an historical sequence of development and styles. Although the book is out of print, copies ought still to be available in large libraries. Particularly interesting is the emphasis laid by the authors on the association of the embroiderer's craft in olden days with those of the weaver, sculptor, painter and other artists.

Lastly in this short chapter we may mention weaving, in the shape of a book designed for the beginner, M E Pritchard's **A short dictionary of weaving** (Allen and Unwin, 1954). This covers the terminology of spinning, dyeing and textiles generally, as well as a guide to different types of loom and the craft of weaving. The illustrations are clear and useful.

MUSEUMS AND ART GALLERIES

10 A LARGE PART of the staple content of museums everywhere consists of products of the arts, and although the idea of collecting precious or significant objects together for the edification and use of scholars and public alike is not new, there is nevertheless perhaps more consciousness today of the wonderful treasures housed in national and public collections than ever before.

It is obvious that the catalogues of contents which all museums make available to users are an instructive source of reference and information, and people seeking to study one of the arts, either as practitioners or collectors, will undoubtedly have early recourse to their own local museums and galleries, wherever they be.

This chapter does not seek to give broad coverage of museum catalogues, but only to mention a few British ones which are of special interest because of the nature of the collections they describe.

First of all, the British Museum in London published in 1962 a general **Guide** to its public services, which gives a succinct account of the scope of this great national institution. This is not only relevant to visitors, of course, but is used by many people in other countries whose field of interest may lead them from time to time to make enquiry of the great storehouses of knowledge throughout the world. Museums exist to reveal and further knowledge, and in doing so they are not bound by narrow concepts of territorial boundary or citizenship. Knowledge should be international.

The elegantly produced **Bulletins** of the Victoria and Albert Museum in London and the Liverpool Public Libraries, Museums and Art Galleries must not be overlooked. The first number of the former was published in January 1965 and it is issued quarterly. Articles, beautifully illustrated, have so far covered English brass inlaid furniture; a hundred years of English silver; Handel at Vauxhall and Florentine embroidery, among others. A cumulative index must be provided eventually to make possible the maximum use of this scholarly and imaginative enterprise. The Liverpool *Bulletins*

76

have been published since 1952, and whilst they are mainly concerned with important acquisitions by the city, they have also dealt with interesting general subjects such as English bookplate styles. Their standard of production is excellent.

The London National Gallery **Reports,** the most elegantly produced of all British museum publications, cover the period 1938-1954; January 1955 to June 1956; July 1956 to June 1958; July 1958 to December 1959; January 1960 to May 1962, and June 1962 to December 1964. The booklets now contain the annual report of the director and full invaluable information regarding the running of the gallery and the problems with which it is confronted.

The **Annual reports** of the Leicester Museums and Art Gallery are always beautifully produced, with photographs of recent acquisitions. The city of York Art Gallery issues a quarterly called **Preview** which describes gallery activities and outstanding purchases. Both these are well worth indexing.

News of exhibitions in London and the provinces can be gleaned from leaflets and posters issued by the Arts Council (which cover their own exhibitions), and the Art Exhibitions Bureau in Suffolk Street, London, which are much more extensive. **Special occasions** —some of the year's important events in Britain—also lists exhibitions and festivals and is published monthly by the British Travel and Holidays Association.

Nor should the **Museums journal** be overlooked. This is obtainable on a subscription basis from the Museums Association. It was first published in 1901 as a monthly but became a quarterly in June 1961. The format was completely changed and many illustrations introduced. Although mainly intended for those concerned with museums and galleries, it has scholarly articles on a variety of subjects and an annual index.

In April 1961, the same association also began a **Monthly bulletin** which gives items of news and notices, especially advertisements for vacant appointments, letters to the editor, appointments, promotions and obituaries, and a very selective list of temporary exhibitions.

The locations, contents and hours of opening of museums and galleries in Great Britain and Ireland can be found from a variety of publications. An annual in soft covers by Index Publishers gives an alphabetical list of buildings under towns, their contents, telephone numbers and hours.

The National Benzol Company issued a booklet on **Museums** by Paul Sharp and E M Hatt in 1964, published by Chatto and Windus, a selective list with generous descriptions and fascinating illustrations.

Her Majesty's Stationery Office published the eighth edition of **Guide to London museums and galleries in 1964.** This is a very handy booklet, well produced and especially well illustrated.

The **Museums calendar** includes a directory of museums and art galleries of the British Isles, together with a select list of institutions overseas. This comes annually from the Museums Association.

The Libraries, museums and art galleries year book (Clarke) was compiled and edited by Edmund V Corbett and issued in a welcome, revised edition in 1964. For professional people this directory is an indispensable standby. More than half the book is concerned with public libraries, but the libraries and museums of Eire are detailed and the museums and art galleries of the United Kingdom. The information given is more detailed here than anywhere else and can be found under place names.

INDEX OF TITLES

ELVILLE, E M : Collectors' dictionary of glass (£8 8s), 49

Encyclopaedia of world art: 15 volumes, in progress, (£224 7s 6d), 11

ESDAILE, K : English church monuments 1510-1840 (21s), 40

ETHERIDGE, K : Stage costume for the amateur, 72

ETTORE, C see Galetti, U and Ettore, C

EVANS, J : Art in mediaeval France 987-1498 (£4 4s), 28
A history of jewellery 1100-1870 (£5 5s), 59

EVANS, M : Costume throughout the ages (40s), 69

Everyman's concise encyclopaedia of architecture (BRIGGS), 44

Everyman's dictionary of pictorial art (GAUNT), 10

FERNALD, M and Shenton, E : Costume design and making (15s), 71

Fine art reproductions of old and modern masters (SOHO GALLERY), 38

FLEMING, J : Scottish country houses and gardens open to the public (25s), 48

FLETCHER, Sir B : A history of architecture on the comparative method for students, craftsmen and amateurs (£4 4s), 43

FLETCHER, C R L and others : Historical portraits 1400-1850 : 4 volumes, 28

FOSTER, J J : Dictionary of painters of miniatures (21s), 33

FRANKFORT, H : Art and architecture of the ancient Orient (£4 4s), 29

FRIEDLÄNDER, M J : Early Netherlandish painting from van Eyck to Bruegel (42s), 37

GALETTI, U and Ettore, C : Enciclopedia della pittura italiana : 2 volumes, 33

GARDNER, A : English medieval sculpture (63s), 40

GARDNER, H : Art through the ages (40s), 26

GARDNER, J S : English ironwork of XVII and XVIII centuries, 74

GAUNT, W : Everyman's dictionary of pictorial art : 2 volumes (50s), 10

Gazette des beaux arts, 20

GERSON, H and ten Kuile, E H : Art and architecture in Belgium 1600-1800 (63s), 27

GIEDION-WELCKER, C : Contemporary sculpture (£5 5s), 41

GLAZIER, R : Manual of historic ornament (15s), 44

GLOAG, J : A short dictionary of furniture (42s), 54

GODDEN, G A : Encyclopedia of British pottery and porcelain marks (£6 6s), 51

GOLDSTEIN, F : Monogram Lexikon, 33

GOMBRICH, E H : The story of art (36s), 26

GRANT, M H : Dictionary of British etchers (30s), 57
Dictionary of British landscape painters (£7 7s), 33
Dictionary of British sculptors, 13th-20th century (50s), 42

Graphis (£6 per annum), 20

GRAVES, A : British institution, 37
Royal Academy of Arts, 37
Society of artists of Great Britain, 36

GREEN, J M C : Period costumes and settings for the small stage, 72

Guide to London Museums and galleries (HMSO), 78

GUNNIS, R : Dictionary of British sculptors (63s), 42

HAGGAR, R G : Dictionary of art terms (35s), 10
editor : Concise encyclopedia of continental pottery and porcelain (£6 6s), 52
see also Mankowitz, W and Haggar, R G

HAINAUX, R and Yves-Bonnat : Stage design throughout the world since 1935 (£6 6s), 72
Stage design throughout the world since 1950 (£7 7s), 72

HAMER, S H see Dalton, R and Hamer, S H

HAMILTON, G H : The art and architecture of Russia (42s), 29

HANNOVER, E : Pottery and porcelain : 3 volumes, 51

HANSEN, H H : Costume cavalcade (25s), 69

HARRISON, M : History of the hat (18s), 69

HARVEY, J : English mediaeval architects (75s), 47

HATT, E M see Sharp, P and Hatt, E M

HAUSER, A : The social history of art : 24 volumes (10s each), 25

HAYWARD, H : World furniture (£5 5s), 53

81

6

NATIONAL GALLERY: Catalogues of paintings, 31
Reports (2s 6d each), 77
New York Graphic Society fine art reproductions (SOHO GALLERY), 38
NORRIS, H: Costume and fashion: 3 volumes (£8 5s), 65
NOVOTNY, F: Painting and sculpture in Europe 1780-1880 (63s), 34

ORPEN, Sir W see Shipp, H
The outline of art (SHIPP), 27
Oxford history of English art (BOASE), 28

PAINE, R T and Soper, A: Art and architecture of Japan (63s), 29
PARKE BERNET GALLERIES New York: Sales catalogues, 17
Pelican history of art (60s-90s per volume), 24
PEVSNER, N: Buildings of England, 45
Picture encyclopaedia of art (73s 6d), 12
PIJOAN, J: History of art: 3 volumes (volumes 1 and 2 40s, volume 3 42s), 25
PLANCHÉ, J R: Cyclopaedia of costume: 2 volumes, 68
PLENDERLEITH, H T: Conservation of antiquities and works of art (70s), 22
PLOMMER, H: Ancient and classical architecture (35s), 44
Portrait index (AMERICAN LIBRARY ASSOCIATION), 18
POST, C R: History of Spanish painting: 12 volumes (prices vary with volumes and some volumes are out of print), 37
see also Chase, G H and Post, C R
PREECE, L see Symonds, M and Preece, L
PRITCHARD, M E: A short dictionary of weaving (18s), 75

RACKMAN, B: Guide to the collections of stained glass (6s 6d), 49
RAYMOND, W: Coins of the world of the 19th and 20th centuries: 2 volumes (85s), 61
REDGRAVE, S and R: A century of painters of the English school: 2 volumes, 35
REES, T M: Welsh painters, engravers and sculptors, 18
Repertoire d'art et d'archaéologie, 18
REWALD, J: History of impressionism (£5), 34
Post impressionism (£6), 34

RICH, J C: The materials and methods of sculpture (87s 6d), 42
ROBERTSON, D S: A handbook of Greek and Roman architecture (50s), 30
ROHRBACH, C see Kretschmer, A
ROSENBERG, A: Design and development of costume: 5 volumes, 69
ROTHENSTEIN, Sir J: The Tate Gallery (£6 6s), 36
ROYAL INSTITUTE OF BRITISH ARCHITECTS: Catalogue of the library, 43

SCHMITT, O: Reallexikon zur Deutschen Kunst-geschichte: in progress, 12
SCHMITZ, H: Encyclopedia of furniture (75s), 53
SEABY, B A Ltd: Standard catalogues of British coins (20s), 61
SELWYN, A: Retail jewellers' handbook (42s), 60
SEMPLE, W illustrator: Scottish tartans (7s 6d), 73
SEUPHOR, M pseud: A dictionary of abstract painting (42s), 33
The sculpture of this century: a dictionary of modern sculpture (90s), 42
SHARP, P and Hatt, E M: Museums (6s), 78
SHAW, H: Dresses and decorations of the Middle Ages: 2 volumes, 69
SHENTON, E see Fernald, M and Shenton, E
SHIPLEY, R M: Dictionary of gems and gemology, 59
SHIPP, H: The outline of art (45s), 27
SIMPSON, F M: History of architectural development: 4 volumes (45s, 35s, 40s, 65s), 44
SKIRA, A: Art editions, 31
Art ideas histories series, 27
Great centuries of painting series, 31
Painting colour history series, 31
SLATER, J H: Engravings and their value (42s), 57
SMITH, H C: Catalogue of English furniture and woodwork, Victoria and Albert Museum department of woodwork, volume 1—Gothic and early Tudor; volume 2 Late Tudor and early Stuart, 53
SNOOK, B: Costumes for school plays (16s), 71
English historical embroidery (16s), 74

SNOWMAN, A K: The art of Carl Fabergé (£6 6s), 60

SOHO GALLERY: Fine art reproductions (£6 6s), 38

SOPER, A see Paine, R T and Soper, A

SORIA, M see Kubler, G and Soria, M

SOTHEBY and co: Sales catalogues, 17

STEPHENSON, M: A list of monumental brasses in the British Isles (30s), 41

STEWART, C: Early Christian, Byzantine and Romanesque architecture (30s), 44
Gothic architecture (35s), 44

STEWART, D C: Setts of the Scottish tartans (70s), 73

STONE, L: Sculpture in Britain: the Middle Ages (63s), 40

STRICKLAND, W G: Dictionary of Irish artists: 2 volumes, 18

The Studio (4s per month), 19

STUDIO: Decorative art in modern interiors (63s), 15

SUMMERSON, J: Architecture in Britain 1530-1830 (90s), 46

SYMONDS, M and Preece, L: Needlework through the ages, 75

TATE GALLERY: Modern British paintings, drawings and sculpture in the Tate by all British artists born in or after 1850: 2 volumes (50s each), 13

TATTERSALL, C E C: A history of British carpets from the introduction of the craft until the present day (42s), 74

TEN KUILE, E H see GERSON, H and ten Kuile, E H

THIEME, U and Becker, F: Allgemeines Lexikon der bildenden Künstler von der Antike bis zur Gegenwart: 37 volumes, 32

TILKE, M: Costume patterns and designs (£6 6s), 67
Costumes of eastern Europe, 66
Oriental costumes, 66
and Bruhn, W: Pictorial history of costume (£6 6s), 67

TIPPING, H A: English homes: 9 volumes, 47

TOMAN, K: Book of military uniforms and weapons (30s), 70

TOY, S: The castles of Great Britain (35s), 48

TRUMAN, N: Historic costuming (25s), 65

TWINING, E F: A history of the crown jewels of Europe (£16 16s), 60

UNESCO: Catalogue of colour reproductions of paintings: 2 volumes (30s each), 39

VAN MARLE, R see Marle, R van

VAVRA, J R: 5,000 years of glassmaking (£4 4s), 49

VICTORIA AND ALBERT MUSEUM: Bohemian glass (7s 6d), 49
Bulletins, 76
Catalogue of water-colour paintings by British artists, 36
Glass tableware (1s 6d), 49
Lists of accessions, 14
department of woodwork: Catalogue of English furniture and woodwork: 4 volumes, 53

VOLLMER, H: Allgemeines Lexikon der bildenden Künstler des XX Jahrhünderts: 6 volumes (£52 10s), 32

WALKUP, F P: Dressing the part (63s), 70

Wallace Collection furniture catalogue (WATSON), 54

Warburg and Courtauld Institute journal, 21

WATERS, A W: Notes on 18th century tokens (14s), 62

WATSON, F J B: Wallace Collection catalogue: furniture (16s), 54

WELCKER, C Giedion see Giedion-Welcker, C

WHINNEY, M: Sculpture in Britain 1530-1830 (84s), 40

WHITE, A V: Making stage costumes for amateurs, 72

WHITING, G: Lace guide for makers and collectors (66s), 75

WHITTICK, A: European architecture in the 20th century: 2 volumes (30s, 42s), 45
Symbols, signs and their meaning (50s), 27

Who's who in American art ($22.50), 13

Who's who in art (£4 4s), 13

WIER, A E: Thesaurus of the arts ($5), 9

85

WILENSKI, R H: Flemish painters 1430-1830: 2 volumes (12 12s), 34
French painting (35s), 34
Modern French painters (£5 5s), 34
WILLS, G: English looking-glasses (70s), 55
WILSON, H W and co: Art index, 18
WITTKOWER, R: Art and architecture in Italy 1600-1750 (70s), 29
Writers' and artists' year book (12s 6d), 16
WYLER, S B: Book of old silver ($4.50), 58

YARWOOD, D: The architecture of England (84s), 45
English costume from the 2nd century BC to 1960 (35s), 66
The English home (52s 6d), 54
The year's art: 64 volumes, 15
YORK ART GALLERIES: Annual reports, 77
YVES-BONNAT *see* Hainaux, R *and* Yves-Bonnat

ZAIDENBERG, A: Art students' encyclopaedia ($5), 11

INDEX OF SUBJECTS